Stiff as a Poker

AND OTHER OZARK FOLK TALES

Illustrations by Glen Rounds

Stiff as a Poker

AND OTHER OZARK FOLK TALES

COLLECTED BY Vance Randolph

WITH NOTES BY HERBERT HALPERT

BARNES
&NOBLE
BOOKS
NEW YORK

TO OTTO ERNEST RAYBURN

Originally published as *The Devil's Pretty Daughter*
Copyright 1955 Columbia University Press

This edition published by Barnes & Noble, Inc.,
by arrangement with Columbia University Press.

1993 Barnes & Noble Books

ISBN 1-56619-090-8

Printed and bound in the United States of America
M 9 8 7 6 5 4 3 2 1

Preface

PARTS of this collection were first published in the *Journal of American Folklore*, the *Southern Folklore Quarterly*, and *Midwest Folklore*. A few items are reprinted from my books *Ozark Mountain Folks* and *From an Ozark Holler*, issued by the Vanguard Press in 1932 and 1933, both long out of print. Others appeared in two pamphlets, *Funny Stories from Arkansas* and *Funny Stories about Hillbillies*, published by E. Haldeman-Julius in 1943 and 1944. I thank the owners of these copyrights for permission to use the material here.

V. R.

Contents

Introduction

IN the Ozark Mountains elderly folk still lead simple lives, without any modern gadgets. They are attached to particular localities, strongly influenced by clan and family backgrounds. The gods of the mountains are not the gods of the valleys. Hillfolk are not like lowlanders. My Ozark neighbors cherish values and prejudices very different from those current in other sections of the United States. Such people do not read much, but live in an atmosphere of oral tradition. They have little material wealth, but more leisure than city dwellers can afford. There is still plenty of time, in the backwoods, to sing ballads and tell tales.

I began to gather Ozark folk tales in 1920. Since then I have lived in many parts of the region, with special attention to isolated and underprivileged communities. Avoiding the progressive people of the towns, I tried to cultivate villagers and country folk, preferably men past middle age. These old-timers did not read the tales in any book. They learned them by word of mouth, just as their parents and grandparents did. Such stories were told in lonely cabins, beside little stills in dark hollows, around midnight campfires on the ridges. I listened to storytellers in taverns and village stores, on the courthouse steps, at the mill while our corn was a-grinding, beneath the arbors where backwoods Christians congregate. Several of my best pieces were recorded in a house of mourning, when we sat up all night to keep cats away from the corpse.

In the early days of my collecting I was accompanied by a young woman who wrote down every word in shorthand as the storyteller spoke. At another period, when the Library of Congress employed me to collect folk songs, we used the Library's recording machine for stories also, and transcribed them from aluminum discs. More often, having neither stenographer nor recorder, I made notes in pencil and typed the story a few hours later, before the notes grew cold. My purpose was to record each tale just as I heard it. No item in this book is an exact literal transcription, but they're all pretty close to the mark. The tales are not retold or rewritten; they are not literary adaptations or re-creations. I did not combine different versions, or use material from more than one informant in the same text.

I have changed proper names whenever it seemed advisable, and translated a few dialect terms. I tried to preserve the Ozark idiom, but made little effort to reproduce the hillman's pronunciation. I blue-penciled a lot of cusswords, because the profanity which adds force to an oral narrative becomes monotonous in print. Many of our finest Ozark yarns are full of obscenities, but I have done no bowdlerizing. My feeling is that these bawdy items cannot be cleaned up without eviscerating them. If a story contains "unprintable" words I omit the whole thing instead of trying to expurgate it.

In choosing the material for this book I followed the storytellers' preference rather than my own. The tales printed here are those which the hillfolk like best and tell oftenest. I am content to string along with the old-timers in this, believing that such samplings should be representative rather than selective.

Some of these stories came to the Ozarks from the highlands of Virginia and Kentucky and Tennessee, at the beginning of the nineteenth century. Many of them are paralleled in European collections, and have been reported by folklore journals on both sides of the water. I have little knowledge of this literature, but my friend Herbert Halpert has supplied important annotations and references. Dr. Halpert knows as much about folk tale scholarship as anybody in America, and his notes add greatly to the scholarly usefulness of this book.

As I have indicated elsewhere,[1] there are many men in the Ozarks today who delight in telling whoppers to the tourists. The fine art of windy-spinning is by no means obsolescent. So long as our summer visitors are ignorant and credulous, the tall tale will continue to flourish. But the items in this book are not regarded as tall tales, and the casual tourist never hears them. These stories belong to an older generation, people whom I knew only in their latter years. The old-timers had little contact with outsiders.

I still record a folk tale occasionally, when the moon is right, but genuine storytellers grow scarcer every year. Of the fifty-nine persons contributing to this book, forty-one have died since 1920. Collectors nowadays do not meet such women as Emma Dusenbury, who astonished John A. Lomax with her songs and stories. My friend Mary Burke remembered many tales, but few were recorded because she despised tourists and rarely spoke to "furriners." City folk seldom appreciate men like Uncle Jack Short, in whose home I lived for more than a year. The late Riley Robertson, who kept a colorful establishment called the House of Lords, knew scores of pioneer tales. Rose O'Neill had lived in all the capitals of Europe, but she spent her last years at the old home on Bear Creek, recalling sprightly legends of Whackerdam and Sowcoon Mountain. My old neighbor J. A. Sturges accumulated a vast fund of up-the-

[1] *We Always Lie to Strangers,* 1951, p. 271.

creek stories, but he isn't around any more. Neither is Sam Mc-Daniels, who laughed his way into the Missouri Legislature, nor "Hotel Charley" Hiatt, whose anecdotes will be remembered after all the prominent citizens are forgotten. Allen McQuary, once famous as the "Plumed Knight from Arkansas," is off to Fiddlers' Green, and may God rest his gallant spirit. Tom Shiras is dead, and so is the inimitable Frank Hembree. These men and women were storytellers of the old school. The new crop is not the same at all. Most of the second-growth Ozarkers have some schooling, and read comic books. Our young people do not care for the traditional tales nowadays. They like radio gags and wisecracks better.

Well, time marches on, and you can't turn back the clock. Literacy has its advantages, electric lights are easy on the eyes, contact with tourists is profitable, concrete highways are convenient, and travel is broadening. A few years more and the younger hillfolk will be thinking and talking pretty much like conventional Americans elsewhere. To those of us who knew the old-timers, the transition is not without a touch of melancholy and regret. We shall miss the storytellers. Their passing closes a romantic and colorful chapter in the history of our country.

V. R.

The Devil's Pretty Daughter

ONE TIME there was a man lived in a fine house, and he owned a big scope of land. Some folks thought he was the Devil, and they used to call him that behind his back. But all the young fellows for miles around wanted to get a job on his place, because he had a pretty daughter named Ruthie-ma-Toothy. The old Devil hired everybody that come

3

along and worked 'em till they was nothing but skin and bones. But nary one of them boys ever got next to Ruthie. She just laughed and never paid no mind to what they said at all.

There was one fellow named Alf Knight worked there seven years, and he bantered Ruthie-ma-Toothy to run off with him. She says he better shut up, because the big black rooster can talk and tell the Devil everything that is going on. So Alf kept out of the rooster's way after that. But he went right on a-bantering her to run off with him. Finally Ruthie saddled two horses, and then she give the big black rooster a bushel of corn. "Let's hit the mountain right now," she says. "Soon as the rooster eats all the corn, he'll tell Pap we're gone."

Alf and Ruthie rode fast as they could, but pretty soon they looked back, and there come the old Devil on his big black horse. He was smelling their track just like a tree-dog follers possums. It looked like the old Devil was going to catch them sure, but Ruthie-ma-Toothy pulled some bramble-briars out of her pocket. "Throw them down in the road behind us," she says, and Alf done it. The bramble-briars took root and growed a mile a minute; they kept on growing till the valley was plumb full, and it looked like a high level prairie. The old Devil had to ride a thousand miles out of his way to get around that briar-patch.

Alf and Ruthie kept on a-riding, and after while they looked back, and there come the old Devil still follering the trail. It looked like he was going to catch them sure, but Ruthie-ma-Toothy pulled three little gravels out of her pocket. "Throw them down in the road behind us," she says, and Alf done it. The little gravels took root and growed a mile a minute; the whole country was covered with loose gravels and quicksand fifty foot deep. There was long chat-piles everywhere, like what

4

they got up around Joplin, only bigger. The old Devil had to ride two thousand miles out of his way to get around that gravel-bar.

Alf figured they had the old Devil beat this time, but Ruthie knowed better. So they kept on a-riding, and after while they looked back, and sure enough there come the old Devil. It looked like he was going to catch them after all, but Ruthie-ma-Toothy pulled out a bottle of water. "Pour it down in the road behind us," she says, and Alf done it. The water took root and growed a mile a minute; the creek busted out of its banks and run all over the country. There was big barns a-floating off down stream, and haystacks with chickens a-riding on 'em. The old Devil cain't cross running water, and he had to ride three thousand miles out of his way to get around that flood.

Alf and Ruthie kept on a-riding, but along the next evening they looked back, and there come the old Devil. He was a-moving pretty slow now, but he was still follering the trail. It looked like he was going to catch 'em soon or late, no matter what happened. Ruthie-ma-Toothy pulled a little Bible out of her pocket. "Throw it down in the road behind us," she says, and Alf done it. The little Bible took root and growed a mile a minute; the whole country was full of paper with holy words on it, and everybody knows the old Devil cain't stand Bibles. He couldn't get through and he couldn't go round, so finally he just give up and went back home.

Alf and Ruthie kept on a-riding, and pretty soon they come to the place where his folks lived. So they went in for dinner, and everybody liked Ruthie-ma-Toothy fine. Next day there was a preacher come along, so her and Alf got married without no more foolishness. She took up piecing quilts and making soap and having babies, and never mixed in no devilment.

5

Everybody for miles around thought Ruthie was wonderful. Alf he thought so too, and him and her lived happy ever after.

What Candy Ashcraft Done

ONE TIME there was a man and woman come a-traveling through the country with a good team and a brand-new Springfield wagon. They was Yankees, and both of them loved money. So they got a fine coffin with silver handles and put it in the wagon. Whenever they come to a big house the woman would rub whitening on her face and then lay in the coffin like she was dead.

The man would go to the door and ask the people if he could sleep in the barn, and then he wanted to put the corpse in the house till morning. He is used to sleeping in barns himself, but he don't want it said that his poor sister has laid a corpse in no barn, because they come of a good family back home and it would break his mother's heart. So the folks would help carry the coffin into the house, and everybody says it is a handsome corpse. Away in the night the woman would get up out of the coffin and unbar the door, so the man could come in. And then they would rob the house and maybe kill all the people besides.

When they come to the old Ashcraft place it was a fine big house, but there wasn't nobody living there only Lige Ashcraft and his wife Candy. They didn't like Yankees much, but no Ashcraft could turn down travelers, and it was coming on to rain anyhow. So they helped carry the coffin into the big hall.

They give the fellow a good supper and offered to let him sleep in the spare room. But he says no, as he is all dirty from traveling. And his poor sister's jewelry and keepsakes are packed in the wagon, so he will sleep out there in the wagon-shed, he says.

Lige and Candy give him the lantern, and then they barred the door and went to bed. After they laid there awhile Candy says, "Listen, Lige, there's something funny about them people." Lige he just grunted. Pretty soon Candy says, "Lige, I could swear I seen that corpse's eye-winker move, right after we set the coffin on them chairs." Lige says it is all foolishness, because he seen thousands of dead Yankees in the War, and their eye-winkers never moved a goddam bit. "You better go to sleep," he says, "because we got to get up early. That poor fellow wants to get a soon start in the mornin', and we must give him a good breakfast." And then Lige he rolled over and begun to snore.

Candy laid there and thought about it awhile, and then she got up easy and went downstairs barefooted. She picked up a hatchet by the kitchen stove, and then she slipped into the hall and hunkered down close to the coffin. After while there come a little noise, and the woman in the coffin set up. She had a gun in her hand, so Candy just swung the hatchet. The Yankee woman fell back in the coffin, and Candy set down on the floor because she was kind of dizzy. Candy hadn't never killed anybody before, and she felt like maybe she was going to faint.

Pretty soon she went back and woke up Lige. When she told him what happened he says she must have dreamed it. But he slipped down to the hall and seen how things was. Then he picked up the hatchet and motioned for Candy to unbar

7

the door. Soon as it swung open the other Yankee come a-sneaking in. Lige just split his head open like it was a pumpkin. The fellow never knowed what hit him.

After Lige lit the lamp, him and Candy just set there awhile, looking at them corpses. Both of the Yankees had pistols and knives under their clothes. The man was wearing a money-belt full of gold, and the woman had three diamond rings in a little sack round her neck. There was a big bundle of greenbacks and silver in the coffin, too. Soon as it got light enough, Lige dug a big hole out in the cornfield and buried the corpses and the coffin with the silver handles. Then he drove off down the road, and after while he come back afoot. Lige never did say what he done with them fine horses and the Springfield wagon, and Candy had sense enough not to ask no questions. She just scrubbed the hall right good and washed the hatchet. Lige wrapped the money and the rings up in a piece of rawhide and put it in a safe place. He showed Candy where the stuff was hid, so she could find it if anything happened to him. And then him and her set down and eat their dinner, just like they always done.

Lige and Candy talked some about going out West, but they never done it. They raised a big family right there on the old farm. The kids all went to school, and one of the boys made a lawyer, and finally he got to be prosecuting attorney. After Lige died Aunt Candy just visited around amongst the children. Whenever they give a party the old lady would dress up just as fine as anybody. She had three gold rings, too, with big diamonds in them.

A Slim Yellow Catfish

ONE TIME there was an old bachelor lived up on the Meramec, and he was the best noodler in the whole country. He caught more fish with his hands than most fellows could get with a big seine. This evening he was feeling around in a black hole under a bunch of horsetail rushes, and he drug out a slim yaller catfish that would weigh pretty near a hundred pounds. The funny thing was how that fish kept a-hollering. Like one of these little squealer-cats they catch out of White River, only louder. It was still squealing when he got it home in the wagon. The rain-barrel was about half full, so he just put the catfish in the barrel with its head down. He figured the water would keep it alive, and next morning he'd sell it to the fellow that run the new hotel.

Along in the night he heard that fish a-flouncing round like a mule kicking in the barn, but he knowed in reason it couldn't get away, so he just went to sleep. When he woke up there was a woman in bed with him. It wasn't none of the neighbor gals neither, but a plumb stranger. She was a right good-looking woman, and they stayed in bed pretty late. Finally he says maybe we better get up, but the woman didn't seem to have no clothes, so he didn't mention it no more. After while he went outside, and the big catfish was gone out of the rain-barrel. It looked like a lot of funny things was happening. The old bachelor thought maybe he was going crazy, but he never said nothing. He just went back to the house and crawled in bed again.

So that's how things went for three whole weeks, and the old bachelor was wore down to a nub. But whenever he got to thinking about some way to get rid of the woman, she would just look at him. She never said a word, only just looked at him, and went right ahead with what she was a-doing. Some women is terrible single-minded, and it looked like there was the Devil to pay and no pitch hot. The old bachelor felt pretty bad, and hungry besides. Everything was going plumb to hell, and he knowed the whole place was a-growing up in weeds, but there wasn't no help for it.

One morning he woke up before daylight, and the woman was gone. He figured she must have went outdoors for a minute, so he just laid there and tried to think. It come in his mind that he could saddle old Maud and ride off through the woods. Maybe he'd leave the whole goddam country, and go to Oklahoma or somewheres away out West. Pretty soon he heard a noise outside, something a-flouncing round like a mule kicking in the barn. When he looked out the door, there was the slim yaller catfish in the rain-barrel, with its tail sticking up and flappin' against the clapboards.

Soon as he seen that fish, the old bachelor run for the barn. He hitched up faster than the boys at the fire station, and pulled out his endgate, and got the rain-barrel in the wagon. One big jump and he was on the seat. Down the lane they went, with the mules at a full gallop and water a-splashing every which way. You'd think he was making for town to sell the fish, but the team took the river road instead. Pretty soon they come to the deep water, and the old bachelor dumped that yaller catfish right back where he got it. The big fish turned round and looked at him just once. Then she flipped her tail, and that was the last he ever seen of her.

The old bachelor never done no more noodling, and he never eat no more fish, neither. He says anything that smells like fish made him kind of sick. But he used to walk down by the river sometimes, particular in the Spring. They say he would set on the bank for hours, a-looking into a black hole under a bunch of horsetail rushes.

Old Wall-Eyes

ONE TIME a fellow started out with a wagonload of beef, and he figured on peddling it to the town folks. He had to pass through the woods where Old Wall-Eyes had his den. Old Wall-Eyes had a mouth big as a churn, and the more he ate the bigger it got. His eyes was big as teacups, and they went round and round. If he run fast his eyes went round fast, and if he walked they went round slow. The closer he got to you the bigger his eyes was, and everybody was afraid of him. But Old Wall-Eyes couldn't climb no trees. He had to just plain run on the ground like a horse, only faster.

When the fellow had just about got out of sight in the woods he heard something begin to squall. He knowed right then that the wagon wheels had woke up Old Wall-Eyes. And pretty soon here *come* Old Wall-Eyes, with his eyes a-whirling round and round. Here he come, just a-tearing up the bushes and a-pitching them behind him.

The fellow took one look, and them little old mules was

a-running for all they was worth. The wagon went a-bumping onto rocks and over stumps and a-splashing through the branch and up the hill lickety-split, with Old Wall-Eyes right behind them, a-getting closer all the time. Here he come, and he was fairly clearing the ground. He was squalling worse than a hungry painter-cat. His eyes was big as saucers, and his mouth was big as a washpan. He was a-tearing up the bushes and a-pitching them behind him.

He come up to the wagon, and the back endgate was out. You could tell he was aiming to jump right square in the middle of that wagonload of beef. The fellow picked up a beef shoulder and throwed it out. Old Wall-Eyes stopped to swaller the beef, and then here he come again. His eyes was big as bread plates, and his mouth as a peach basket. He was just a-tearing up the bushes and a-pitching them behind him.

So the fellow throwed out a hindquarter of beef. Old Wall-Eyes caught it, and swallered it on the run. His eyes was a-turning round like two big crocks, and his mouth was big as a washpot. He was just a-tearing up the bushes and a-pitching them behind him.

The fellow he chunked out the whole half of the beef that was left, but Old Wall-Eyes didn't stop for long. He just gobbled it up and here he come again, with his eyes a-rolling like two cotton baskets and his mouth open big as a fireplace. He just kept a-stomping up the bushes and a-coming on.

Finally the fellow reached down over the dashboard and unhooked the traces of one mule. Then he jumped a-straddle and away they went, while Old Wall-Eyes swallered up the other mule just like a chicken snake would swaller a hen egg. His eyes was big as two cookstoves, and his mouth was big as the wagon gate at the cotton-house. He had it wide open, too,

12

and he was a-gooshing like a big old river hog. "Gooshie-gooshie-gooshie-gooshie!" is what it sounded like. He sure was a-clearing up the timber and a-coming on.

The fellow could feel Old Wall-Eyes a-blowing right down his shirt collar. It looked like Old Wall-Eyes was going to swaller the man and the mule and the gear and all for sure, when what do you think? The fellow seen a big old pine tree, and he sure didn't lose no time a-climbing it. Old Wall-Eyes just went round and round and round that pine, a-tearing up the bushes and a-pitching them behind him.

But the fellow was safe, because Old Wall-Eyes couldn't climb no trees. He had to just plain run on the ground like a horse, only faster.

The Cuckoo's Nest

ONE TIME there was a horse-trader that was away from home a good deal. His woman just stayed around the house and never went to the tavern. But there was a young fellow named George Borrow that would come and see her in the night, when her husband was not home. The young fellow scratched on the window glass, and she would get up to let him in.

The horse-trader never suspicioned nothing, until one night he come home unexpected. Pretty soon the young fellow sneaked up and scratched on the window glass. Soon as she heard it the woman begun to sing:

> Go way from my window, my honey, my love,
> You cain't fly here, my sweet little dove.
> My heart's in my breast, an' the cuckoo's on the nest,
> Go way from my window, my honey, my love.

The horse-trader heard the scratching and he heard the singing. It didn't take long to figure out how things was. But he just let on like he was asleep, and never said nothing.

Next morning he went off down the road and told everybody he figured on being gone three or four days, but the same evening he come back home through the woods and got in bed. Pretty soon the young fellow sneaked up and scratched on the window glass. The horse-trader put his hand over the woman's mouth so she couldn't say nothing, and then he begun to sing:

Go way from my window, you son-of-a-bitch,
I hope you rot off with the seven-year itch.
Your name it is Borrow, I'll kill you tomorrow,
Go way from my window, you son-of-a-bitch!

The woman didn't say one word after that, and neither did the horse-trader. Next morning she fixed him a fine breakfast, and after he eat it he went down to the place where the young fellow stayed. But the folks says George had went to town. So the horse-trader rode into town, too. He looked in the boardinghouse and the poolhall and the saloon, but George Borrow was plumb gone. The fellow at the depot says he left out on the train and bought a ticket plumb to Kansas so he could work in the wheat harvest.

So then the horse-trader rode back home, and he paddled his wife's bottom till she couldn't set down for a week. He says if there is any more of this cuckoo-on-the-nest business he will kill all the young fellows for five miles around, and no questions asked. And after that he rode off to the County Fair in Durgenville.

Nobody here ever seen George Borrow again, and it was damn good riddance. The folks all say that the horse-trader and his woman got along pretty good from that time on and never had no more trouble.

Aunt Kate's Goomer-Dust

ONE TIME there was a farm boy named Jack and he wanted to marry a rich girl that lived in town, but her pappy was against it. "Listen, Minnie," says the old man, "this feller ain't house-broke, scarcely! He's got cowdung on his boots! He cain't even write his own name!" Minnie didn't return no answer, but she knowed what Jack could do, and it suited her fine. Book learning is all right, but it ain't got nothing to do with picking out a good husband. Minnie had done made up her mind to marry Jack, no matter what anybody said.

Jack wanted to run off and get married regardless, but Minnie says no, because she don't figure on being poor all her life. She says we got to make Pappy give us a big farm with a good house on it. Jack he just laughed, and they didn't do no more talking for awhile. Finally he says well, I'll go out on Honey Mountain tomorrow, and see what Aunt Kate thinks.

Aunt Kate knowed a lot of things that most folks never heard tell of. Jack told her what a fix him and Minnie was in, but Aunt Kate says she can't do nothing without silver. So Jack give her two dollars, and it was all the money he had. Then she fetched him a little box like a pepper-duster, with some yellow powder in it. "That's goomer-dust," she says. "Don't get it on you, and be careful not to get none on Minnie. But you tell her to sprinkle a little on her pappy's pants."

Late that night Minnie dusted some powder on the old man's britches, where he had hung 'em on the bedpost. Next morning he broke wind right at breakfast, so loud it rattled the pictures on the wall and scared the cat plumb out of the kitchen. The old man thought it must be something he et. But pretty soon he ripped out another one, and it wasn't no time at all till he was making so much noise that Minnie shut the windows for fear the neighbors would hear it. "Ain't you goin' down to the office, Pappy?" says she. But just then the old man turned loose the awfullest blow-out a body ever heard, and he says, "No, Minnie. I'm goin' to bed. And I want you should fetch Doc Holton right away."

16

When Doc got there Pappy was feeling better, but pretty white and shaky. "Soon as I got in bed the wind died down," he says, "but it was terrible while it lasted," and he told Doc all about what happened. Doc examined Pappy a long time and give him some medicine to make him sleep. Minnie follered Doc out on the porch, and Doc says, "Did you hear them loud noises he keeps talkin' about, like somebody breakin' wind?" Minnie says no, she didn't hear nothing like that. "Just as I thought," says Doc. "He just imagined the whole thing. There ain't nothing wrong with your pappy only his nerves."

Pappy slept pretty good, on account of the medicine Doc give him. But next morning, soon as he got up and put his clothes on, he begun to break wind worse than ever. Finally he fired off a blast that sounded like a ten-bore shotgun, so Minnie helped him back in bed and sent for the doctor. Doc give him a shot in the arm this time. "Keep that man in bed," says he, "till I get Doctor Culberson to come over and look at him." Both of them doctors examined Pappy from head to foot, but they couldn't find nothing wrong with him. They just shuck their heads, and give him some more sleeping medicine.

Things went along like that for three days a-running, and finally Doc says Pappy better stay in bed all the time for awhile, and take medicine every four hours, and maybe he would be happier in a institution. "Put me in the asylum, just because I got wind on the guts?" yelled Pappy. And with that he begun to raise such a row the doctor had to give him another shot in the arm.

Next morning Pappy set up in bed a-hollering how the doctors are all damn fools, and Minnie says she knows a fellow that can cure him in five minutes. Pretty soon Jack come a-walking in. "Yes, I can cure you easy," he says, "but you got to let me and Minnie get married, and give us one of them big farms." Pappy wouldn't even speak to Jack. "If this half-wit cures me," he says to Minnie, "you can have any goddam thing you want." Minnie walked over and stirred up the coals in the fireplace. Soon as it got to burning good, Jack took the tongs and threwed Pappy's britches right in the fire.

When Pappy seen them pants a-burning he was plumb speechless. He just laid there weak as a cat, and Jack marched out like a regular doctor. But after while the old man got up and put on his Sunday clothes. He never broke wind, neither. Minnie fixed him a fine breakfast, and he et every bite of it and never even belched. Then he walked round the house three times, without feeling no gas on his innards. "Well, by

God," he says, "I believe to my soul that damn fool did cure me!" On the way down town he stopped in to see Doc Holton. "I finally got well, without no thanks to you," says he. "If you had your way, I'd be in the crazy-house this minute!"

Soon as he got Doc told, Pappy went over to the bank and deeded his best farm to Minnie. He give her some money to buy horses and cows and machinery. And so her and Jack got married, and they done all right. Some folks say they lived happy ever after.

The Baby in the Cradle

ONE TIME there was a fellow stole a pig from his neighbor. The neighbor seen he was a pig short, and suspicioned what become of it, so him and the sheriff went to the fellow's house in the night. There wasn't no light, but the sheriff hammered on the door so loud you could hear the pictures falling down off the wall inside. Finally the fellow opened the door and he says, "For God's sake don't make so much noise, as we got a mighty sick baby here."

The sheriff says we have come to get the pig you stole from this man. But the fellow says I never stole no pig, and I ain't got no pig, and don't talk to me about pigs while our baby is dying of the smallpox! Soon as he heard *smallpox* the neighbor run off down the road for fear he would catch it. But the sheriff says, "Smallpox don't scare me none, because I have had the smallpox, and it's my job to search this here premises." So he looked all over the place, but he didn't find no pig.

After while the sheriff give up, and then he come back to

the house and says, "Let me look at that baby, and I will soon tell you if it's got smallpox or not." But the fellow had the baby in the cradle, and he says you can hunt pigs all you want, but pulling quilts off'n my sick baby is something else again, because the night air will kill it sure. The sheriff is paid to fight road agents, says he, and not go around a-murdering people's children.

While they was a-cussing the baby begun to wiggle under the covers, and pretty soon it hollered "Oink, oink!" like that. So the sheriff jumped quick and pulled off the quilts, and there was a pig laying in the cradle. It wasn't no baby at all. But when the sheriff turned round to arrest the fellow that stole the pig, he was plumb gone. He had done slipped out the door and run off in the dark, and it wasn't no use to look for him. So then the sheriff carried the pig back where it was stole from, and that's all there is to the story.

Setting Down the Budget

ONE TIME there was a fellow batching all by himself, and he was on his way home from town. It was Saturday, so he had bought him a nice piece of hog-liver, a sack of cornmeal, a little poke of sugar, two fine big onions, a package of salt, and a box of pepper. He was walking along the road with all this stuff in a budget, and thinking what a fine Sunday dinner he was going to have.

All of a sudden he seen a squirrel run up a big tree into a hole. The fellow figured maybe there was young squirrels in the hole, and young squirrels are mighty good with dumplings, so he set down his budget and climbed up to see about it. About halfway up the tree the fellow happened to look down, and there was a red fox upset the budget and run off with the liver. "That's what a man gets for bein' greedy," says he. "I ought to have knowed there wasn't no young squirrels in January, anyhow." So he slid back down the tree and picked up his budget.

He went on down the road a piece, and pretty soon he seen where somebody had been digging under a big rock. The fellow figured maybe the bank robbers had buried some money there, and money is a mighty good thing to have, so he set down his budget and cut him a stick. Just as he got to poking around in the hole, the fellow happened to look around, and there was a big wolf upset the budget and run off with the cornmeal. "That's what a man gets for lovin' money," says he, "an' I ought to have knowed there wasn't no bank robbers out here in January, anyhow." So he throwed the stick away and picked up his budget.

He went on down the road a piece, and when he come to the footlog he seen something white behind the willows, and heard a lot of splashing and squealing. The fellow figured it was some girls in swimming, and peckerwood girls are mighty good, so he set down his budget and busted right through the bushes. Just as he come out on the gravel bar he happened to look back, and there was some pigs upset the budget into the creek. The sugar and salt was melted, and the pepper just floated off on top of the water. "That's what a man gets for bein' too horny," says he, "an' I ought to have knowed there wasn't no gals a-swimming in January, anyhow." So he put his clothes back on and picked up his budget.

The fellow was pretty near home by this time, but there wasn't nothing left in the budget only one onion. "Well, maybe I can scrape enough meal out of the barrel to make a pone," says he. "Last Sunday I didn't have nothing but bread for dinner, and tomorrow I'll have bread with onion on it. Things are getting better, and maybe next week I can get hold of some salt!"

Some folks might think that fellow was a fool for setting his budget down three times and losing his dinner that way. But he was smart enough to be satisfied with what he did have and look hopeful to the future. Which is more sense than most people have got these days.

The Soot on Somebody's Back

ONE TIME there was a pretty girl and her parents was dead, so she kept house for her six brothers. They was away from home a good deal, but she just barred the door and went to bed. But all of a sudden she woke up one night, and there was a man in bed with her. He was a great big fellow, and he was stark naked. The poor girl tried to fight him off, but she couldn't do nothing. It was black dark, and the man never said a word, so she didn't know who he was. And when it come morning he was gone, and the door was barred same as always. She didn't see no way a man could get in the house.

The next night the same thing happened again. The girl tried to fight him off, but he was too strong and she couldn't do nothing. And when it come morning the door was barred again, the same as always.

The third night she mixed some soot in a dish of grease, and set it right by the bed. And when the man come in, she took some of the grease in her hand and put it on his back.

Next day the brothers come home and she told them how some fellow has got the best of her. They looked around mighty careful, and the oldest brother found where somebody had loosened two wide boards in the floor, so that's how he could get into the house. They all says they will kill whoever done it, and she told 'em the man has got a big wart on his back. And so the brothers took their guns and rode all around the neighborhood. Whenever they seen a young fellow they would make him take off his shirt, but they never did find nobody with a wart on his back.

When they come home that evening the girl got the oldest brother in the shed-room by himself, and she asked him to take off his shirt. Soon as she seen there wasn't no soot, she told him just what happened, and she showed him the dish with the black grease in it. And she says, "Did any of them fellows that you caught today have soot on their back?" The oldest brother says no, but you could see he was studying mighty serious about something.

Pretty soon the oldest brother says, "Well boys, let's go swimming." So all six brothers went down to the river and they was gone a long time, but only five of 'em come back. The other fellow was plumb disappeared, and none of the neighbors ever seen him again. The rest of the brothers never said one word to anybody, and neither did the girl. Things like that do happen sometimes, even in the best families, but there ain't nothing to be gained by talking about it.

23

Grave Robbers

ONE TIME there was two ornery fellows that would do most anything for a dollar, and finally they got so low down they hired out to a doctor. Their business was to steal corpses. The night after a burying they would go to the graveyard and dig up the dead man, and put the dirt back with the flowers on top and all, so nobody couldn't tell the difference. Then they would put the corpse in a wagon and haul it to the medical school at Kansas City. A good fresh corpse would bring twenty-five dollars, and twenty-five dollars was a lot of money in them days.

It was a dark night, and pretty cold with snow still on the ground, when they come to a tavern. So they tied their team to the hitch-rack and went in to get a couple of hot toddies. The corpse was wrapped up in canvas and covered with straw in the back of the wagon. While them no-goods was a-drinking in the tavern, along come a farm boy afoot. He was pretty drunk, so he just crawled into the wagon-bed and laid down. Of course, he didn't know there was a corpse under the straw.

Pretty soon the two grave robbers come out, and they had a bottle of whiskey. Neither one of them seen the farm boy that had went to sleep in the wagon. They just drove on down the road, and every so often they would take a drink out of their bottle. It wasn't long till they got to swapping lies and laughing and slapping each other on the back. Just as they was about to finish the bottle, one of 'em turned around and

24

hollered to the corpse, "Git up, old stiff, an' have a snifter!" The farm boy had pretty near slept off his liquor by this time, so he set up with a jerk. "Don't care if I do," says he.

Well, sir, them two fellows was scared pretty near to death. They both yelled loud as they could, and jumped out of the wagon, and run off through the woods. One of them tore uphill on the right side of the road, and the other one slid down a bank and run through the creek on the left. The farm boy just set there with his mouth open. He figured both of them teamsters must have went crazy. That's what he told the sheriff next day, anyhow. "I could hear them fellers a-hollering for a long time," says he. "They kept a-gettin' fainter an' fainter, but they was still a-hollering," he says.

The dead man's kinfolks was pretty goddam mad when they found the corpse under the straw in that wagon. Them Starbuck boys was all for hangin' the grave robbers, but they never did catch up with them, so far as anybody could find out. The folks took the deceased back home and dusted him off, and people from all over the country come to the burying. That there corpse had the best of it, all down the line. There ain't many fellows, even in Jackson county, that gets two big funerals.

Round the Campfire

ONE TIME there was a bunch of cowpokes a-setting round a campfire. After they et supper, Uncle Jim Bangs seen a fellow name of Sotweed Larkin that was always a-scratching himself, and he says, "Sotweed, tell us one of them windy stories of yourn." The fellow just kind of wiggled for a minute, and then he started to saw 'em off a whopper. "Well, one time there was a bunch of cowpokes a-setting round a campfire. After they et supper, Uncle Jim Bangs seen a fellow name of Sotweed Larkin that was always a-scratching himself, and he says, 'Sotweed, tell us one of them windy stories of yourn.' The fellow just kind of wiggled for a minute, and then he started to saw 'em off a whopper. 'Well, one time there was a bunch of cowpokes a-setting round a campfire. After they et supper, Uncle Jim Bangs seen a fellow name of Sotweed Larkin that was always a-scratching himself, and he says, 'Sotweed, tell us one of them windy stories of yourn.' The fellow just kind of wiggled for a minute, and then he started to saw 'em off a whopper. 'Well, one time there was a bunch of cowpokes . . .'

Yellow Bread

ONE TIME there was a fellow named Job Eskin, and he come a-walking up to where the ladies was giving a dinner-on-the-ground at the Methodist Church. Job was a ragged old peckerwood and pretty dirty, but you can't turn people away from a church sociable, no matter if he puts any money in the hat or not. They had fried chicken and vegetables and pies and all the trimmings, but Job didn't touch nothing but Mary Weatherman's yellow poundcake. He just cut off slice after slice and put butter on it. You wouldn't believe that a skinny little old man could eat so much, unless you seen it with your own eyes.

Pretty soon it looked like Job was going to eat the cake plumb up, and the ladies was getting desperate. So they ask him won't he please sample the fried chicken and the nice beat biscuits. "Thank you, ma'am," says he, "but you just save them things for the high-toned folks. This here yaller bread is good enough for me." In the early days we lived on cornbread mostly, and biscuits made out of white flour was something extra fine. Country folks didn't have biscuits only on Sundays, or when company was a-coming. Job was a good soul, but he didn't know much.

Finally one of them Ledbetter girls whispered something in Job's ear. He looked considerable set back, and after that he didn't gobble no more poundcake, but just et chicken and biscuits like the rest of the boys. Poor Mary Weatherman was plumb sick. "I don't care about my cake bein' gone," she says, "and I don't mind men actin' like hogs, because that's their nature. It's what that old feller *said* that's a-killin' me!" And with that she begun to giggle, and acted like she was goin' to throw a fit, so she had to be took home in the buggy.

Mary Weatherman was kind of upset for about a week, and then she come out of it and bustled round same as ever. But she stayed away from the Methodist dinners after that. And so did poor old Job Eskin.

False Faces in Missouri

ONE TIME there was a fellow named Rufe Yenowine that worked on a newspaper in Arkansas. Every time somebody robbed the bank or anything like that Rufe would write a fine story about how it happened. He was a good hand at such as that, because he knowed all the whores and gamblers and congressmen and policemen and fellows that had got in trouble with the law. Them people would tell him lots of things, because Rufe had sense enough to keep his mouth shut about where he got it. The stories he wrote was printed in big newspapers at Little Rock and Kansas City and even St. Louis. The only thing wrong with Rufe was that he always drunk too much on holidays.

There was one Fourth of July he got on the bus and went to Missouri. When he woke up in the big hotel his bottle was gone, so he come down to the bar. Soon as he got to feeling better Rufe walked out in the street, and a big truck pretty near run over him. Things went from bad to worse all day, because the policemen up there didn't know him. When Rufe finally got back home he was still goggle-eyed, and he set down to write a piece for the paper about how things are in the Puke Territory. He says in the story that the people up in Missouri all go around with false faces on, like these here masks that kids wear for Hallowe'en.

The fellow that run the paper was kind of rattled that day, because of one thing and another, and so they printed Rufe's story just like he wrote it. The home folks thought it was a good joke, and lots of big Oklahoma papers printed it, too. But the people that lived up around Joplin begun to send in letters how it is a outrageous lie, because nobody in Missouri wears false faces. There was so many letters come that finally the fellow that run the paper got mad. He says Rufe will have to apologize and tell the citizens it was a misprint.

So next week Rufe wrote in the paper that everybody makes mistakes, and maybe there is some boys and girls in Missouri that don't wear false faces. "But I still think it's a good idea," he says. The Pukes was madder than ever when they read that. "What do you mean, it's a good idea?" says a fellow in Neosho. "We don't *need* no goddam false faces, I tell you!" And a lady at East Elsey wrote how she is coming down there and horsewhip Rufe, and maybe burn the newspaper office, too.

The fellow that run the paper kept on a-grumbling about the letters from Missouri, because some of them was downright vulgar. And one fellow sent a telegram, all the way from Jefferson City. Finally Rufe says to hell with people if they can't take a joke, so he quit the job and went out West somewheres. They say he done fine, too. But if Rufe ever went up into Missouri again, the home folks never heard tell of it.

The Peddler Wanted Fish

ONE TIME there was some folks named Dunlap, and they run a hotel. The building didn't amount to much, but they sure set a good table. The victuals wasn't doled out in little dishes, like at them restaurants in town. No sir, the Dunlaps just had big platters of everything, family style, and a body could eat all he wanted. Salesmen used to come from all over the country, even if they had to drive fifty mile out of their way.

A big peddler walked in one day and set down to the table with the rest of the folks. There was fried chicken and roast beef and baked ham and boiled 'taters and cabbage and sparrowgrass and fried eggs and cornbread and hot biscuits and watermelon preserves and three bowls of jelly and two kinds of pie, but this here stranger turned up his nose at everything. "Pass the fish," says he. Old man Dunlap looked considerable set back, but he always tried to be polite. "I'm sorry," he says, "but we ain't got no fish today, because this is a Thursday. You come around tomorrow night, and we'll have a fine mess of fried catfish."

The peddler didn't make no answer. He just nibbled at a biscuit with some jelly on it and took two or three bites of pie. Then he got up and walked over to the front of the dining room, where the Dunlaps had a fine goldfish bowl. All of a sudden he reached into the bowl and snatched out one of them

30

big goldfish. He started eatin' it, and you could hear his teeth a-crunchin' right through the bones! Folks just set there goggle-eyed, with their mouth open. Pretty soon the fellow grabbed another goldfish, but people was getting up from the table by that time, and some of them upset their chairs. Old man Dunlap begun to cuss something terrible, and the peddler kind of sidled out the door. It's just as well he did, because old man Dunlap was pretty mad. Some citizens seen the peddler walking down the street. He still had part of a goldfish in his hand, like a kid with a stick of barber-pole candy.

The folks found out afterwards that the whole thing was a joke them fool salesmen had rigged up. The peddler didn't really eat no goldfish, but just two dummy fish they had whittled out of raw carrots. Old man Dunlap was so goddam mad that everybody was afraid to tell him for pretty near a week. And even when they did explain it, the old man didn't cool off much. He says to hell with jokes that spoil people's dinner. And nobody hadn't better make light of Mistress Dunlap's cooking neither, if they know what's good for them.

Right down to this day, according to them drummers, it ain't safe to mention goldfish around the Dunlap Hotel.

Spanish Gold

ONE TIME there was a fellow named Hamilton Sipes went over in the Indian Territory and married up with a Choctaw. Three or four years later he come back home, and he had a buckskin map marked with pokeberry juice. This here map showed how to find a buried treasure in a cave, right close to where Ham was raised.

The way Ham told it, a bunch of Spaniards come up here in the early days, and they had gold by the bucketful. Some say they had stole it down in Mexico, but maybe they dug the stuff out of the ground right here. Anyhow, they sure had it. When the Indians jumped on them they hid the gold in a cave, and then they tried to get away down the river, but the redskins killed every last one of 'em. It is against Choctaw religion to mess with dead men's gold, but one of the warriors made this here map, and it was handed down in his wife's family. Ham got hold of it some way, while he was a-livin' in the Territory.

When he got back home, Ham just visited round amongst his kinfolks for awhile. Then one day he borrowed a pick and shovel and started out to get the gold. There was seven pony-loads of it, according to the old story, and Ham figured he'd be a rich man. He found the cave hole all right, and there was the three turkey tracks carved on a rock, just like it was on the map. Ham stopped to rest right outside the cave, when all of a sudden he heard a noise, and here come a terrible big rock a-bouncin' down the mountain. He throwed himself under a ledge, or it would have killed him sure. He just left the pick and shovel lay, and went over to Zeke Mosier's place. Poor Ham was scared so bad he couldn't eat no supper, and he had the dry shakes all night.

Uncle Zeke tried to tell him there ain't nothing to be scared of. It's in the nature of a rock to roll down hill, he says. All them big boulders in the river bed must have fell off the mountain sometime. "That narrow shave you had yesterday was just a accident," says Uncle Zeke, "and it wouldn't happen again in a thousand years." Ham knowed this was true, but he had lived with the Indians too long. He couldn't forget them old Choctaw stories about what happens to fellows that dig up dead men's treasure.

It was pretty near a week before Ham come back to the cave, and this time Uncle Zeke tagged along. Just as Ham went to pick up the shovel, a copperhead bit him on the wrist. It wasn't no time till his arm was swole plumb to a strut, and he was a-suffering something terrible. Uncle Zeke hitched up and took him into town, and the town doctor give him medicine with a big needle. He finally pulled through, but it was touch-and-go for awhile. And Ham says them Indians ain't such fools as some folks think, and the gold can lay there till hell freezes solid for all he cares.

Some other fellows went and dug in the cave, and nothing happened to 'em. But they didn't have no map, so naturally they never found the gold. Ham's money was all gone by this time, and he couldn't get no credit at the store. He got to thinking how lots of folks has been snakebit right in their own back yard, when they wasn't looking for no treasure at all, but just picking up chips or something. And there wasn't nothing spooky about rocks rolling down the mountain neither, when you come to think about it sensible. So finally Ham says he will make one more try for that there gold.

It was a terrible hot day when Ham and Uncle Zeke started out. When they got to the cave Ham set down just inside the entrance and spread his map out on a flat rock. All of a sudden it got so dark he couldn't hardly see the pokeberry marks on the buckskin. The sky turned plumb black, and then come a terrible roaring up the holler. "Cyclone!" says Uncle Zeke, and they both throwed theirself down on the floor of the cave. The air was full of big trees and branches for a minute, and

33

then it was all over. Ham and Zeke wasn't hurt, but they was covered with dust, and the buckskin map was gone. The cyclone had blowed it plumb away.

Neither one of them fellers said a word till they got back to Zeke's house and took a couple horns of whiskey to clear the dust out of their throat. Then Zeke begun to grumble about the map being lost. "It ain't what you might call lost," says Ham. "I reckon it was just took back where it come from." And the next morning Ham Sipes was gone too, and we never did hear from him no more. The folks always figured he must have went back to the Choctaws over in the Territory.

Bessie and the Eggs

ONE TIME there was a girl that wasn't right bright, but she was always trying to help her maw. Bessie done pretty near everything wrong, though. She would bust the dishes when she tried to wash 'em, and maybe throw the dishwater right on the floor instead of out in the yard. One time she put carpet tacks in the pickles, instead of cloves. The only thing she could do good was gether the eggs. It seems like Bessie knowed eggs was easy broke, and she never cracked a one. But she couldn't get it through her head that dishes was easy broke, too. And there wasn't nobody could learn her nothing, because she wasn't right bright.

The sky got terrible dark one evening, and Bessie's maw told her to go fetch the eggs before it set in to raining. So Bessie put on her fascinator and taken the basket, and then

34

she started for the chicken house. It was out by the barn, and the barn set back quite a piece from the cabin.

All of a sudden the wind begun to roar like a freight train on the Chadwick Branch. Then here come hay and branches and shingles and milk crocks, and a lot of things you couldn't tell *what* they was. Bessie's maw knowed it was a cyclone, and she run and opened the door to holler Bessie back. "Lord a mercy!" she says, and the door was blowed clear off'n the hinges and went a-kitin' off through the woods along with the other truck. Bessie's maw give up when she seen that. She just went in the setting-room and prayed. Pretty soon the roaring eased off, and the wind kind of died down. Then it got lighter in the southwest, and the cyclone was over.

The old woman was a-crying all this time, because the barn

was plumb gone, and she figured poor Bessie must have got blowed away off somewheres so they'd maybe never even find what was left of her.

But Bessie wasn't hurt a bit. She was a-standing right where the chicken house used to be, a-grinning like she was real pleased about something, with the egg basket in her hand. "The chicken house flopped its wings and took off like a buzzard, Maw," she says. "But I sure held onto these here eggs, just like you told me. There ain't ary one of 'em cracked, neither!"

Horn Eats Horn

ONE TIME a man was accused of some bad crime, but he never done it. That didn't make no difference, though. The soldiers come after him, and he took to the woods. He pretty near starved to death. They was crowdin' him awful close, so he climbed up a big tree and hid in a bunch of grapevines, same as a possum. It didn't do no good, because one of them soldiers seen him. They could shoot him down, or they could fell the tree and catch him that way. He knowed he didn't have no chance to get away, so he just slid down a vine and give himself up.

Some of the soldiers was for killing him right now, but they finally decided to take him before the big high judges. They figured on puttin' him through some kind of a trial, and then hanging him. But everybody was a-riddling in them days, and they was awful good at it. They all got to talking as they rode along, so pretty soon somebody says if this fellow can tell us a riddle we can't answer, we'll turn him loose. He thought about it awhile, and then he says:

> Horn eat horn, up a white-oak tree,
> If you unriddle this, you can hang me.

They all scratched their heads, but nobody couldn't figure it out. Some of 'em grumbled a good deal, but finally they give up and says if he can prove it's a regular riddle they'll let him go free.

"Well, my name's Horn," says he. And the soldiers wagged their heads, because they knowed that already. So the fellow went on: "Yesterday I found a cow's horn, and I was so hungry I just gnawed like a dog does a bone. Then I took a rock and busted it up, and roasted some of the pieces. The fire softened it up some, and I was eatin' horn when you treed me in that big white-oak."

The soldiers made him empty out his pockets, and sure enough they found some chunks of burnt horn, with tooth marks on it. So they turned Horn loose, and that's all there is to the story.

A Hunter Calls His Shots

ONE TIME some of the boys went duck hunting on White River, and there was a flour salesman from Kansas City says he wanted to come along. So the boys took the best blinds for themselves and left the city fellow setting in a bunch of grass on a little island. They thought it was a good joke, because they knowed he wouldn't get no ducks

37

there. And he had to stay till they come after him in the boat, because the water was so deep he couldn't wade out.

The drummer set there pretty near six hours, and he wasn't too happy, but there wasn't nothing he could do about it. When the boys come for him he didn't say much, but he seen they all had plenty of sprigs and mallards and other big ducks, while he didn't have nothing. He never seen a wing all day but two little hell-bent teals and a bunch of mud hens.

After supper the whole gang went down to the tavern and took a few drinks, and everybody was a-bragging how they was the best shots on the river. Pretty soon the city fellow says all the ducks he seen was flyin' high, and his gun wouldn't fetch 'em that far off. The boys laughed at this, because they had give him a twelve-gauge Parker with thirty-inch barrels, both full choke. And then he says well, maybe the gun's all right, but the shells they're a-makin' nowadays ain't no good. And so the boys laughed again, because he was using regular duck-loads like the rest of them, and they didn't have no trouble getting ducks. "Lead costs a lot more'n it used to," says he, "an' I believe the cartridge companies are a-skimpin' us on shot."

The boys laughed louder than ever when they heard that, and Lem Collins says, "Let's see one of your hulls." The city fellow fished a shell out of his huntin'-coat pocket. "Just read that printing on the top wad," says Lem. So the fellow put on his specs and looked careful. "It says 3½ drams of powder," says he, "and 1⅛ ounces of number fives. But it don't say *how many* shot, and that's what I'm interested in. You got to have lots of shot to get them high-flyers."

So then they all got to talking about how many shot it takes to weigh 1⅛ ounces. Some figured about 100, but most of 'em thought it must be 500 anyway, and maybe more. "Well," says Lem, "there's one way to find out. Let's each man chip in ten dollars, and then we'll *count* the goddam shot. The fellow that guesses closest takes the money." And so everybody says all right.

Lem took his knife and cut open a shell and dumped the number fives out into a whiskey glass. The bartender done the counting, and they all watched like buzzards. It finally come out 200 even. And when they looked at the cards, the salesman had guessed 200, so they give him the sixty dollars. The boys set around and thought about it for awhile, and finally one of 'em says, "How come you guessed *exactly* how many shot there was in that there hull?"

The city fellow grinned. "Well," he says, "you boys left me on that goddam island, and there wasn't no ducks to shoot at. I didn't have nobody to talk to, nor no cards to play solitaire. How do you reckon I put in my time?"

The boys just looked at one another, with their mouth open like a widder-woman's pig. But nobody had anything to say. And pretty soon they all went to bed, so that is the end of the story.

Andy Coggburn's Song

ONE TIME there was a bunch of fellows got together, and they was called Bald Knobbers. Whenever anybody done something that wasn't right, the Bald Knobbers would ride out with masks on their face and whip hell out of whoever it was, or maybe hang him. There was a young fellow by the name of Andy Coggburn, and they took him out one night and give him a terrible whipping. After that Andy made up a song about the Bald Knobbers, and him and his friends got to singing it all over Taney county. They sung it to the tune of "My Name Is Charles Guiteau," which was a new song in them days. Charles Guiteau was the fellow that killed President Garfield. Some of Andy Coggburn's verses went like this:

There's one big Bald Knobber
Who is a noted rogue,
He stole from Joseph Bookout
Some sixteen head of hogs.
Walked boldly in the courthouse
And swore they was his own,
He stole them by the drove, boys,
And horsed 'em over home.

There is another Bald Knobber
Who rides a pony blue,
He robbed old Nell Macully
And Mister Thompson, too.
He taken all their money
And from them rode away,
And now the highway robbers
Is the big men of the day.

There is one big Bald Knobber
Whose name I will expose,
His name is Nat N. Kinney
And he wears his Federal clothes.
He tries to boss the people
And make them do his will,
There's some that does not fear him,
But others mind him still.

To raise a Bald Knobber excitement
I made a splendid hand.

40

I don't fear judge nor jury,
I don't fear any man.
And if they want to try me
They've nothing else to do,
I'll take my old Colt's Patent
And shoot a pathway through.

The more the boys sung that song the worse things got, and the Old Blue Gobbler was just a-frothing at the mouth. They called Nat Kinney the Old Blue Gobbler, because he was still strutting around in blue clothes like he had wore in the Yankee army. Finally old Kinney run into Andy Coggburn at the schoolhouse one night, and shot him dead. Some folks claim it was a fair fight, because Andy had a gun in his hand. But Andy's friends told a different story.

Two or three months after that Sam Snapp come a-riding into Kirbyville. Sam was a friend of Andy Coggburn, and he was a-humming the Coggburn song. He wasn't singing the words, but just a-humming the tune. A Bald Knobber named Wash Middleton was standing by the store, and he told Sam not to sing no such a blackguard song as that. Sam he kept right on a-humming, and pretty soon Wash shot Sam and killed him. Poor Sam didn't have no weapon, only a little pen-knife in his pants pocket.

The Old Blue Gobbler always claimed he disbanded the Bald Knobbers when Governor Marmaduke threatened to send the soldiers down to Taney. But folks was still getting whipped out of the country, so Kinney's crowd could buy up their farms cheap and steal their stuff. Andy Coggburn laid a-moldering in his grave, but plenty of the boys was still singing Andy Coggburn's song. Some of them sung it right in the street, and their friends a-standing by with pistols cocked, so nobody wouldn't try to stop the music.

41

Finally a fellow by the name of Billy Miles beat Kinney to the draw. Shot him four times with a 44 Colt, and killed him right now. The honest people was mighty glad when they heard the Old Blue Gobbler was dead, and the Springfield newspaper says it was good riddance. They buried old Kinney up on Swan Creek somewhere, without no stone on his grave.

These kids that has growed up lately never even heard of the Bald Knobbers, but the old folks ain't forgot. And there's people right here in town that sing Andy Coggburn's song sometimes, when they get to thinking about how things was in the early days.

The Dumb-Bull

ONE TIME there was a fellow lived on a little farm away up the river. He kept talking how the woods was full of panthers and catamounts. He says he seen their tracks all over the place and heard them squalling in the pineries every night. So finally some regular hunters took their dogs and went out to see about it. They camped on a gravel-bar three nights, and didn't hear nothing but hoot owls. The truth is that wolves is pretty common yet, and so is foxes, and maybe a bobcat comes through the holler once in a while. But there ain't been no panthers in that country for twenty years.

But this here scary fellow kept right on talking about panther tracks. The old hunters just laughed, and they got to calling him "Panther Pete." But the folks up that way are mostly damn fools, and pretty soon everybody for miles around was hollering about panthers, and some people was scared to step out of their own house after sundown. Some of the town boys got together one day and made a dumb-bull. They just took a barrel and stretched rawhide over one end, like a drum. Then they cut a hole in the rawhide and fixed a leather string with rosin on it, to pull through the hole. The noise a dumb-bull makes ain't very loud, but it sounds terrible deep and dangerous. You can hear it a mile off easy, if the wind is right.

They hauled the dumb-bull out there in a wagon, and a couple of boys carried it up on the hill, just above Panther Pete's house. They could see him out in the field, and his wife and another woman was hoeing in the garden. There was three or four children a-playing round. When the boys pulled the string on that there dumb-bull, Pete jumped about six foot high and looked all round like a pop-eyed rabbit. Then he took out for the house, but the womenfolks had done gathered up the kids and got there ahead of him. They barred the door, too. The fellow hollered and cussed and pounded, but them women was so scared of panthers they wouldn't let him in. Just when he was about to bust the door down, the boys turned the old dumb-bull loose again. Next thing they knowed Panther Pete scrambled up onto the roof, and he was hollering down the chimney for Lucy to fetch him the gun.

After he hollered himself plumb out of breath, Pete crawled down to the edge of the roof, and one of the women opened the door just a crack. Maybe she figured on letting her man into the house, or else she was aiming to pass the gun up to him. But them fool boys pulled the string again, and the old dumb-bull roared louder than ever. The door slammed shut quick as a wink, and Pete scampered up onto the ridgepole again. The boys laid low for awhile, but every time Pete started to come down the old dumb-bull would let out a whoop, and he'd go a-scuttlin' back up to the peak of the roof. They kept it up till plumb dusk, and then they carried the dumb-bull back to town. The last they seen of Panther Pete he was still setting on top of his house, a-cussing the womenfolks because they don't come out and fight like a man.

Ever since that day, Pete carries a gun all the time, and he can't be talked out of it, neither. Some of the folks tried to tell him about the dumb-bull joke, but Pete just laughed in their face. And he says you can't fool me about them things, because I have studied the varmints from childhood up, and I know a panther's holler when I hear one. It sure don't sound like no boys fooling with rawhide in a rain-barrel, he says.

Just a few years back the float-trip people seen him out there a-plowing, with a long six-shooter hanging down and his belt full of big brass cartridges. The guides told the tourists how the feud had broke out again, and them farmers was killing each other every Saturday, and all kind of foolishness. But the home folks knowed it was just old Pete, fixing to protect his family from them man-eating panthers up in the pineries.

Gunpowder in the Stove

ONE TIME there was a fellow kept a little crossroads store, and the store was always full of people but they did not buy nothing. Some of them loafers would be there by daylight, and they would stay till dark. They just played checkers and swapped lies all day long. Some of them would buy a dime's worth of cheese and crackers about noon, but mostly they fetched along their own cornbread and a piece of meat from home. They cluttered up the store so bad that cash customers couldn't get in, hardly. And there was two or three that would make some smart-aleck remarks when a woman come in the store. And every once in a while they would get to scuffling around, and maybe bust something. It got so the place looked like a boar's nest all the time, and the fellow that run the store couldn't figure out no way to get rid of them loafers.

Well, a stranger come riding in one day on a paint pony, and one of them Puke saddles with the horn sticking up like a plow handle. He was wearing a gun tied low, and cowboy boots. So the loafers begun to make jokes about how the grasshoppers has eat up Oklahoma, but the stranger just looked at them contemptuous, and didn't return no answer. "Give me three pounds of gunpowder," he says to the storekeeper. The fellow that run the store weighed out the powder, and everybody seen him put the powder in a paper sack and tie it with red string. The stranger bought some tobacco and paid for it, and then he picked up the powder and started to go out.

The storekeeper says, "Ain't you forgot something?" but the fellow just looked at him. "You forgot to pay me for the powder," says the storekeeper. The stranger says he has paid once, and that is enough. "You must be mistaken, Mister," says the storekeeper, and then he says, "Boys, did you see this gentleman pay me for the powder?" The loafers all shuck their heads, and one fellow spoke up, "I seen him pay you for the terbacker, but I didn't see him pay you for the powder," he says.

The stranger just reached over and opened the door of the hot stove. "You jaspers is all in cahoots," he says. And with that he threw the big sack of gunpowder into the stove and slammed the door shut. The loafers all jumped and run, and they pretty near wrecked the store building a-getting out. They didn't stop till they was away down the road, and then they just stood there a-shivering. They figured the store would be blowed sky-high any minute. Pretty soon they seen the storekeeper come to the door, and he threw the loafers' overcoats right out on the ground. He threw out their little budgets of corn-bread and meat, too.

After while one of the boys sneaked up and looked in the window. There was the storekeeper and the stranger a-setting by the stove, eating sardines and crackers. And every little bit they would slap each other on the back and laugh about how them bums was scared out of a year's growth. "I don't see how they done it," says one of the loafers, "they must have switched sacks on us some way." And another fellow says, "It has got so citizens can't come to the store nowadays, without having some fool tricks played on them. From now on," says he, "I aim to take my business somewheres else." And so all the loafers picked up their overcoats and went down to the livery barn. The storekeeper says it is damn good riddance, and he don't want that class of trade anyhow.

Slipping Through the Keyhole

ONE TIME there was a orphan boy named Harry, and he went to work for old Gram Wallace and her two daughters. They had the best farm on the creek, but the house didn't amount to much. It was just a one-room log cabin, with three beds in it. Gram slept in the best bed all by herself, the two girls slept together in another big bed, and Harry had a shakedown over by the door. They set a good table, and treated Harry all right, but he was kind of worried about something.

Every once in a while Harry would wake up in the night, and all three of them women was gone. But the door was still barred and the window shutter hooked on the inside. And then when he got up in the morning, there was Gram and the girls in their beds. Harry knowed there was something funny a-going on, but he couldn't figure out how they done it.

Finally one night he just let on like he was asleep, and he seen them women get up and put a pan of water on the hearth. They washed their face in the water, and each one says, "Out I go and touch nowhere!" And with that all three of 'em flicked right up the big old chimney. After they was gone Harry got up and washed his face. "Out I go and touch nowhere!" says he. Before you could bat a eye he was up the chimney and flying through the air. Pretty soon he lit in a big pasture, where all kind of people was fiddling and dancing and having a regular picnic. Some of them women didn't have enough clothes on to wad a shotgun. Harry liked it fine, and everybody treated him wonderful. But all of a sudden a rooster crowed, and the next thing Harry knowed he was back home in bed. Gram Wallace and the girls was in their beds too, and time to get up and do the chores.

After breakfast the youngest girl winked at Harry, and she says, "Did you have a good time last night?" Harry told her he sure did. "Well," she says, "you sneak off and meet me down by the sheep-shed pretty soon." So Harry done it, and him and her had more fun than you could shake a stick at. He went down to the sheep-shed every day after that. "This flyin' up chimneys ain't nothing," she says. "You stick with me, an' I'll show you how to slip through keyholes." And so they used to get into stores of a night, and eat all the candy they wanted. Sometimes they would go right into people's houses, and maybe knock something over and scare hell out of the folks. One time they seen a man in bed with his wife, and so they waited awhile and then both of them busted out laughing. The man jumped up and started to get his gun, but they was out of the keyhole before he could see who it was. Harry never did learn the words just right, so whenever they went to slip through a keyhole the Wallace girl would tell him what to say, and he just mumbled it after her.

Everything went fine till the night they slipped into old man Gifford's house. Old man Gifford was on the school board, and so the pretty schoolmarm stayed at his place. Her door was open and Harry got kind of rattled. He forgot all about the Wallace girl and jumped right in bed with the pretty school-marm. But the schoolmarm could tell right away it wasn't old man Gifford, so she begun to holler. She hit Harry on the head with her shoe and knocked him plumb senseless. The Wallace girl was mad, so she just slipped out the keyhole by herself.

Poor Harry sure was in a bad fix. Old man Gifford like to beat him to death, and then tied him up with rope. Next morning the sheriff come and put him in jail.

Harry laid in jail for pretty near a month. He just set there day and night trying to think of the words you say to slip through a keyhole, but he couldn't do it. The night before they was going to have the trial, the Wallace girl come and said the words for him, so he got out. But she was still pretty mad, and she says a man like him ain't fit to slip through keyholes or anything else. She say he better high-tail it clear out of the country before morning, or else old Gram Wallace will say some words to turn him into a boar hog. Harry never returned no answer. He just took off through the woods, and nobody in that country ever laid eyes on him again.

The county officers made a terrible holler about Harry getting out of jail, with the door still locked and all. Some said old man Gifford must have paid the sheriff to take him out and kill him. But old man Gifford says if he wanted to kill Harry he'd have done it the night the fellow was ketched in a criminal act, and not called the sheriff till afterward. So most folks figured the Wallace girl let him out through the keyhole and turned him loose, just like the old story says. It sounds more reasonable that way.

There's Bigger Fools Than Tildy

ONE TIME there was a fellow named Tom and he had it all made up to marry a girl name of Tildy. But when he went to see her, she just set in the smokehouse a-crying. There was a butcher knife stuck in a rafter, and she says, "Oh Tom, wouldn't it be awful if that knife was to fall down and kill our baby?" Tom he just looked at her. "We ain't got no baby," says he. "Yes, but what if we was to get married and have one," she says. "You don't need to worry," says Tom, "because if anybody is such a fool as that I wouldn't marry her on a bet." So then Tom he walked off down the road, and Tildy just set there and bawled louder than ever.

Pretty soon Tom come to where a bunch of folks was camped beside the creek, and he heard something go *thump, thump, thump* like that. And there was a fellow putting on his pants. He had the pants hung on a rope between two trees, and he was trying to jump into them both legs at once. Tom looked at the fellow awhile, and then he went on down the road.

Pretty soon Tom come to a church house, and there was a woman a-pushing against the front of it. She says her little boy has got the runnin' flux, and he made a mess on the front steps accidental. And now she is trying to push the meetinghouse back, so the people that come to church won't see the mess on the steps. Tom he looked at the woman awhile, and then he went on down the road.

Pretty soon Tom come to a little cabin, and there was an old woman kept a-running in and out the door. She held up her apron like she was carrying something, but there wasn't nothing in the apron. She says she has got the floor scrubbed, and now she is packing in sunshine to dry it. Tom he looked at her awhile, and then he just shuck his head and went on down the road.

He thought about it a long time, and then he says to himself all these people is a bigger fool than Tildy, and it looks like I might go further and fare worse. So then he turned round and went right back where he started from. Tildy was still worried about the butcher knife a-falling on the baby, but Tom says, "Never mind, honey, because everything will be all right." And pretty soon him and Tildy got married, and they lived happy ever after.

On Breadtray Mountain

ONE TIME there was some town people coming along the old road on Breadtray Mountain, and they heard a lot of hollering off to the left. The moon was a-shining, but nobody couldn't see where the noise come from. It sounded like men and women was a-fighting with corn knives. You could hear yells and grunts and groans, and every once in a while they would drop their corn knife in the gravels. Then somebody just breathed heavy and moaned like they was a-dying. As soon as things quietened down, the crickets and katydids begun to sing again, like nothing had happened.

The people just stood there in the road and looked at each other. They knowed in reason there wasn't no settlement on the mountain, so they says it must be wild hogs a-fighting up the slope somewheres. It didn't sound like hogs, though. It sounded like men and women a-killing each other with big knives. There was one fellow figured maybe the goddam place is haunted, but the rest of 'em just laughed at him. Folks that live in town nowadays listen to so many lies that they can't trust their own ears no more, and don't believe nothing. So that's why they thought it must be hogs.

The truth is that hogs was never known to bed down on Breadtray, because there ain't nothing there for 'em to eat. The racket them people heard was something else again. The old settlers say that a long time ago there was a bunch of Indians lived on the mountain. There wasn't no regular folks here in them days, till a bunch of white men come up the river. Some of 'em was a-riding horses, and the Osages hadn't never seen nothing like that before, so they figured these fellows must be angels from heaven. But the fact is they was just soldiers, and Mexican soldiers at that. Or maybe Spanish, according to the old story.

The Osages give the white men the best victuals they had and sent all the prettiest young girls up there to wait on them. But the soldiers was a tough lot, and it wasn't no time till they had the squaws' clothes off and was carrying on something scandalous. They didn't treat them Osage girls right. When the Indians seen that, they knowed them fellows wasn't angels at all, but just natural men. So they come with bows and spikes and tommyhawks. The soldiers fought, but they didn't have no chance. Pretty soon the Spaniards was all dead. The Osages killed the squaws too, because they figured a girl that had laid up with foreigners wasn't no good.

Next day they washed the dead girls and buried them Osage style, but just left the soldiers lay there for the buzzards. And for a long time after that there was Indians walking around with iron shirts on and carrying them long swords with silver crosses on the handle. They had finger rings, too, and little medals strung round their neck. Some folks claim the Spaniards buried a lot of gold around here some place, but nobody ever found it. If them fellows had any gold the Osages must have took it, like they done the other truck.

All that business of Spaniards and Osages a-fighting is just a story about something that happened a long time ago, and maybe it ain't true at all. But the hollering that folks hear on the mountain is different. There must be fifty people a-living right here in this county that has heard them noises plain. Mostly good Christian folks, too, and they ain't a-lying. Just go up on old Breadtray any night in the Fall, when the moon is right, and you'll hear something a-hollering and a-grunting and a-groaning. And every once in a while comes a clatter like somebody a-dropping their corn knife in the gravels.

We know it cain't be live men and women. It cain't be hogs, neither, and there ain't no wild varmints in this country that could make such a racket. The old-timers stick to their tale about the Osages a-killing Spaniards. But everybody has got a right to their own opinion. As for these here newcomers, let 'em believe whatever they goddam please.

Little Thumb and the Giant

ONE TIME there was a fellow named Little Thumb, and he used to slip into the old giant's house pretty often. There was good things to eat over there, and he liked the giant's wife besides. The giant's wife told him to stay away, or else the old giant would kill him sure. But Little Thumb just laughed, and kept right on a-coming.

It blowed up a big rain that evening, and Little Thumb

knowed the giant would be home any minute. But he went to bed in the spare room anyhow, and pretty soon he heard the old giant a-coming. So Little Thumb slipped out of bed and run to the fireplace. There was a pile of chunk-wood beside the hearth. Little Thumb put some wood in the bed and pulled the quilt over it. Then he hid over in the corner where it was dark, and he laid right still. Pretty soon here come the giant, and busted the wood in the bed with his big club.

When Little Thumb come down to breakfast next morning the giant was mighty surprised, because he figured Little Thumb was dead sure. "Did you sleep good last night?" says he. "Yes, I slept fine," answered Little Thumb, "only there was a rat run across the bed, an' kind of slapped me with his tail." The giant just set there and goggled at him. Little Thumb didn't pay no attention, and the old giant thought this fellow is a lot tougher than he looks.

The giant eat breakfast enough for twenty men, and pushed big platters of stuff over to Little Thumb. "Eat every bite of it," says the giant, "I cain't stand to see good victuals go to waste." Little Thumb was ready for this, and he had a big sheepskin sack under his clothes. He let on like he was eatin', but just slipped most of them victuals into the sack. "By God," says the old giant, "I believe you can eat as much as me!" Little Thumb just grinned at him, and shoveled in some more ham and a couple dozen fried eggs, and washed them down with a gallon of coffee.

"Eatin' is easy," says Little Thumb, "but I can do somethin' else that you cain't do. You'd be scared to try it, even." The giant begun to holler how he ain't scared of nothing, but Little Thumb says, "Give me that knife, an' I'll show you." So the old giant give him the knife. Then Little Thumb stood up and

54

cut the big sack open right through his jacket, shirt and all. It made a big hole, and pretty near fifty pounds of ham and eggs and biscuits and coffee sloshed right out on the table.

"Well, by God!" says the giant, "if you can do it, so can I!" And with that he grabbed the knife and cut himself wide open. So then the old giant begun to bleed like a stuck pig, and pretty soon he fell down dead. And from that time on Little Thumb just went to the giant's house whenever he felt like it, and done whatever he wanted to.

Bang Away, My Lulu!

ONE TIME there was a young fellow married a fine woman, but he would not stay home of a night. He was always sneaking off to see a no-good hussy named Lulu, that he had went with before. His wife raised hell about it, but she would not leave him because she didn't believe in no divorce. Also, she did not like to live at home with her folks, and there wasn't no other place for her to go. Another thing was, she didn't want people to think that some cheap floozy has took a man off'n her. And maybe she was kind of crazy about the young fellow, besides.

So finally she went and told her Aunt Sophie. The old woman says there is ways to take care of things like that, but it is kind of spooky and dangerous. She says it would be better just to let your fool husband go, as he ain't no good anyhow. But the girl says all she wants is to keep her man away from Lulu. "I don't want to kill nobody," she says, "but I will do anything short of a killin', no matter if it is spooky or not."

Aunt Sophie took chalk and drawed a big ring on the floor, and she killed a black chicken, and fixed up some other things that had to be done. And she got a boy to go in the night and steal one of Lulu's petticoats. Aunt Sophie tied the petticoat onto a pillow. Then her and the young fellow's wife took turns a-pounding it with a club. The girl thought it was all foolishness, but Aunt Sophie made her keep right on a-pounding the pillow to the tune of "Bang Away, My Lulu."

When the young fellow got to Lulu's house she was laying on the bed. She says, "That goddam wife of yours come here with some old woman, an' they throwed me down an' beat me something terrible." The fellow says, "Nonsense!" but Lulu pulled up her clothes and showed him how she is plumb black-and-blue. So the young fellow went home and says, "What do you mean, going around beating people with clubs? I never heard of such a thing," he says, "and you will disgrace the whole family!" And then his wife says, "It must be you are going crazy, because I have not been out of this house all day, except over to Aunt Sophie's." The young fellow went over to see Aunt Sophie, and she told him the same thing.

Next morning Aunt Sophie fetched the petticoat over and tied it onto a pillow. Then her and the young fellow's wife took turns a-pounding it and singing "Bang Away, My Lulu." When the young fellow come home he says, "Well, poor Lulu is beat pretty near to death, with blood running down her legs, and I hope you are satisfied." And his wife says, "I have not set foot out of this house all day, and Aunt Sophie has been right here with me." The young fellow went and asked the neighbors, and they all told him it was the God's truth.

Next day Aunt Sophie and the young fellow's wife beat the petticoat again, and clear over in the other end of town Lulu raised such a holler that somebody called the sheriff. When he got there Lulu was a-prancing around yelling that two women was whipping her, but the sheriff could see that she was all alone in the house. So he figured Lulu must be crazy drunk or else taking some kind of dope, and he locked her up in the jailhouse. A lawyer made the sheriff turn her loose that night. Lulu got right on the train and went to St. Louis. She didn't come back, neither.

57

The young fellow never did find out just what happened, but it kind of scared him. He stayed pretty close to home after that, and him and his wife got along all right.

The Marshal in the Barrel

ONE TIME there was a bunch of outlaws over in the Cookson Hill country, and they captured a United States Deputy Marshal. Oklahoma was kind of tough in them days, and it was called the Territory. They didn't have no sheriffs at all, just a lot of United States Deputy Marshals a-riding out of Fort Smith. Them marshals was all gun-fighters and terrible dangerous to fool with, but the outlaws caught this fellow asleep and jumped on him before he could wake up.

Most of them outlaws wanted to hang the marshal, or else burn him alive. But one fellow says my goodness, gentlemen, don't you know there's a law against killing marshals? We better just put the son-of-a-bitch in a barrel and leave him on the prairie. If the damn fool wants to stay in there and die it's his own fault, and nobody can't blame it on us, he says. So they put the marshal in a old salt-barrel and nailed it shut, and then they rode away a-laughing.

It looked like the marshal was a gone gosling. But pretty soon some wild cattle come around, lickin' the barrel for salt. A big steer was a-standing with his tail right next the bunghole. The marshal pulled in a few hairs at a time very careful, and he got the end of the steer's tail inside the barrel before the critter noticed anything. Then the marshal give a pull and held onto the tail with both hands. The steer begun to beller and run, with the barrel a-bouncing along behind him. The marshal held on, because he knowed it was his only chance.

The big old steer kept a-buckin' and a-bellering, and the marshal was bruised up something terrible, but he still held on. Pretty soon they come to Kickapoo Prairie, and two hunters seen the steer a-running with a barrel fast to its tail. So they got on their ponies and come over to find out what was going on. Soon as the marshal heard them he turned loose of the steer's tail. Then he begun to kick with his boots and holler "Help! Help!" as soon as the barrel stopped rolling.

The two hunters come up close and listened awhile, but they didn't know what to make of it. The marshal thought maybe they was more outlaws, so he didn't tell 'em he was a marshal. He just kept a-hollering that he was a white man, and he wanted out of the barrel. Finally one of the hunters stood back with his buffalo-gun cocked, while the other one knocked some hoops loose and busted the barrel open. The marshal come a-crawling out, but he had got skinned up pretty bad, and the blood run into his eyes so he was plumb blind at first.

As soon as he could see, the marshal knowed them two hunters was all right. And when they found out who he was, the hunters took care of him the best they could. He just laid around camp for a few days, and then he got well enough to ride back to the settlement. But the marshal was terrible nervous for a long time after that, and they do say he'd puke like a dog every time he seen a salt-barrel.

One Thing They Can't Sell

ONE TIME there was a young couple that was religious and hard working, but they had a lot of bad luck. The berries didn't hit, the cutworms got the tomatoes, and the corn burnt up three years in a row. They couldn't pay the interest on the mortgage, so finally they lost their farm. The stock and household plunder went too, and it was a pretty sad business.

The young folks saw their machinery sold, piece by piece. Then the furniture was auctioned off, even their old quilts and blankets. Then the neighbors begun to buy the pots and pans in the kitchen. The girl stood it as long as she could. Then she went out behind the barn and cried like a baby.

Pretty soon the husband come out there too, and put his arm around her shoulders. "Well," says he, "they've took everything we had except the little spotted cow, an' now they're a-sellin' her. But there's one thing they *cain't* sell, an' that's our faith in the Lord an' Saviour Jesus Christ." He drawed a long breath. "An' God damn their lousy souls to Hell!"

Heading for Texas

ONE TIME a girl that lived up on Horse Creek got married, and they was going to stay with her folks for a few days. The girl's pappy was an ornery old cuss, and he hid under the fresh-married couple's bed. The young folks didn't know he was there, so they just shut the door and blowed out the light.

"Listen, honey," says the young feller, "I'd like mighty well to ask you somethin'."

The girl says for him to go ahead, and she'd sure give him a straight answer.

"Well," says he, "I want to know if you ever laid up with any other boys, before I come along."

The girl wasn't expecting no such a question on her wedding night, but she answered right up, "Of course I didn't!"

"Oh, well, it don't make no difference," says he, "but I was just thinkin' that you sure missed a lot of fun." The young feller kind of yawned, and then he says, "Naturally the boys likes them pretty gals best. I reckon you didn't have no chance."

The girl set right up in bed, and she was so mad she didn't hardly know what she was a-saying. "Didn't have no chance!" she hollered. "Listen, you son-of-a-bitch, the boys has been chasin' me like pigs after a pumpkin ever since I could show hair! Why, I was a-sleeping with the biggest men in this county before you dried out behind the ears!" The young feller got up and put on his clothes. "Well, I orter have knowed it," says he.

61

Then he jerked on his boots. "I'm a-headin' for Texas," he says, and down the road he went.

Pretty soon the girl's mother come in to find out what had went wrong. They done considerable cryin' an' cussin', but finally the girl had to explain how it happened. The old woman shuck her head. "You sure was a fool to tell him that," she says. "Why, I bet your old pappy has asked me that same question a thousand times. But do you think I told him about all them fellers I used to run around with? What a man don't know won't hurt him, is what I always say."

The old man was layin' quiet under the bed all this time, but when he heard what Maw said he let out a roar like a wild hog and turned the bed plumb over. "Git out of my way!" he yells. "I'm a-headin' for Texas, too!" and down the road he went.

Them two women just set there a-blackguarding each other till both their husbands was plumb out of sight.

How Toodie Fixed Old Grunt

ONE TIME there was a farmer and his wife lived in a little old cabin, right at the edge of the big timber. They had three daughters that was the prettiest girls for miles around. But the folks was awful poor, because the old man couldn't work much, and it was mighty hard for them to keep their skillet greasy.

An old bachelor named Grunt lived down the road a piece. He says he was tired of living by himself, so he married the oldest girl. She didn't want to marry old Grunt, but the folks talked her into it. He had a good farm and a fine big house, and money in the bank besides.

Things went along all right for about a year, and then all of a sudden old Grunt was raising hell all over the neighborhood, because he says his wife has run off with a peddler from Missouri. So then he married the next-to-the-oldest girl. She didn't want to marry old Grunt, but the folks talked her into it. He had a good farm and a fine big house, and money in the bank besides.

Things went along all right for about a year, and then old Grunt's second wife showed up missing, and he says she has run off with a cowboy from Oklahoma. So then he married the youngest girl. She didn't want to marry old Grunt, but the folks talked her into it. He had a good farm and a fine house, and money in the bank besides.

The youngest girl was named Toodie, and she had a boy friend name of Jack. When old Grunt and Toodie went uptown to get married, Jack searched Grunt's house, and he found where the two sisters was killed and throwed in a old cistern. So Jack hid in the bushes, and when Toodie come back he told her, "Old Grunt killed your sisters, look out he don't kill you."

Pretty soon Toodie and old Grunt had words about something, and he says, "You're my wife now, an' you got to mind whatever I say." Toodie she sassed him right back, and old Grunt says, "You better look out, or I will do you the same as I done them other fool girls," and he pulled out his big old knife. "I'm goin' to kill you right now," he says, "an' put you down the cistern!"

Toodie was fixed for him with both hands full of pepper, and all of a sudden she threwed it right in old Grunt's eyes. Old Grunt begun to beller and slash around, but he couldn't see nothing because his eyes was blinded with pepper. Jack come out from where he was a-hiding, and hit old Grunt with a stick of wood. And then him and Toodie wrastled old Grunt down and cut his head plumb off. It served him right, too. So they throwed him down the cistern, and worked pretty near all night a-filling the whole thing up with rocks. And then they put dirt on top, and Toodie planted flowers, so you couldn't tell if there had ever been a cistern on the place.

About three weeks after that Toodie told everybody her husband has run off and left her. She says she can't stay in a big house like that all by herself, and she got the old folks to move in with her. Then after awhile they needed a hired man to help with the work, and so Jack he moved in too.

Things went along all right for a while, and then the old folks died off. Toodie had a good farm and a fine big house now, and money in the bank besides. So her and Jack got married, and raised a big family, and they all lived happy ever after.

The Infidel's Grave

ONE TIME there was a rich infidel died, and the folks buried him without no preacher. Nobody said a prayer, even. That's what the infidel told 'em he wanted, and they done everything just like he said.

The night after the funeral some neighbors got to talking about it, and a old woman says if anybody was to walk on that grave at midnight, the infidel will reach right up and grab 'em. But a girl named Betty Ream just laughed right in their face. She says a infidel's grave ain't no different than anybody else's grave.

So then the boys wanted to bet she is scared to go out there by herself, at midnight. Betty says it is all foolishness, but she will go just to show 'em. And one fellow says, "If there ain't nobody with you, how will we know you was there?" The young folks had been a-playing croquet, and Betty says, "Fetch me that stake with the red rings painted on it, and one of them mallets." So the fellow done it. "You just go over to the buryin' ground in the morning," says Betty. "You'll find the stake drove right in that infidel's grave, and the mallet a-layin' close by."

It was about half-past eleven when Betty rode off down the road. She had the croquet stake in her hand, and the mallet was tied on her saddle. Two of the boys cut across the pasture unbeknownst, and they seen Betty go in the graveyard. They waited a long time, but she never come out. Them boys wouldn't go no further by theirself, but they run to the tavern and got some more fellows and a couple of lanterns. When the crowd come back they found Betty Ream a-layin' on the infidel's grave, and she was dead as a doornail.

Betty had hunkered down and drove the stake, all right. But girls wore big wide dresses in them days, and the moon was behind her, so it throwed a big black shadow in front. That's how come she drove the stake right through the edge of her skirt. The folks figured that when Betty went to get up,

the dress held her fast to the ground. Maybe she thought the infidel sure enough did reach up out of his grave to grab her. Whatever happened, it scared Betty so bad that she died right then and there.

Doc Holton says she must have a bad heart, and maybe wouldn't live long anyhow. But that didn't make the folks feel no better. Betty Ream was mighty good company, and everybody thought a lot of her. It's kind of sad for a young girl to die that way, just on account of some foolishness.

Jack and the Sack

ONE TIME a fellow named Jack done something pretty bad. Some say he killed the Mayor, or raped the Mayor's wife, or maybe he just stole the Mayor's saddlemare. Anyhow, it was against the law. The posse caught him in the big timber south of Doomsbury. They tied him up in a big sack, and two soldiers was told off to drown him in the river.

The soldiers stuck a long pole through the top of the sack, so they could carry it on their shoulders. Pretty soon they come to a tavern. It was a terrible hot day, and dry. So the soldiers just left the sack a-setting by the road and went in to drink some beer. Jack hollered out that he wanted some beer too, but they did not pay no attention.

Poor Jack couldn't see nothing, but he could hear all right. So whenever anybody come along the road he begun to holler, "I won't do it! I won't do it!" Pretty soon a farm boy stopped,

67

and he wanted to know what it is that Jack won't do. Jack says, "These goddam soldiers are taking me to marry the rich man's daughter. But I won't do it! I want to marry Polly Brown!"

The farm boy thought about it awhile, and then he says it wouldn't be no use to marry Polly Brown, because she just works in the tavern and she hasn't got no money. "My gosh," says he, "I wish somebody would give *me* a chance to marry the rich man's daughter!" But Jack says there's things in this world that money won't buy, and Polly Brown suits me right down to the ground. And he says if you want to marry the rich man's daughter, just untie the rope and let me out of here. Then I will tie you up in my place, and them damn fools will never know the difference.

So the farm boy untied the rope and let Jack out. And then the farm boy got in the sack, and Jack tied the rope just like it was before. Pretty soon the soldiers come out of the tavern. They put the pole on their shoulders and went on down the road. When they got to the ferry the farm boy knowed something was wrong. He begun to kick and holler, but the soldiers did not pay no attention. They just throwed him in the river and went on back home.

About a week after that the two soldiers seen Jack in the tavern, and one of them says, "That boy is a dead ringer for the outlaw we drownded." The other soldier looked at Jack pretty careful. "Well," he says, "the people in this country is all kinfolks, and they breed around regardless just like rabbits. Pretty near every man you see is somebody else's cousin, and lots of 'em brother and sister even, so they all look like peas in a pod," says he.

The other fellow thought about this awhile and seen how sensible it was, so he wagged his head solemn like a old-field schoolmaster. Then the soldiers just went on a-drinking their beer, and never paid no more attention.

The Woman in the Bed

ONE TIME there was a fellow traveling afoot, and when night come he was awful tired. He seen a cabin with a light, and when they let him in there was five men a-playing cards. There was lots of money on the table, and them gamblers looked kind of wild and dangerous. They had long hair, and most of them was wearing big guns in plain sight.

The traveler asked if he could stay all night. The gamblers looked kind of funny for a minute, and then they says he could sleep with a woman in a double bed. But he mustn't touch her because she is in poor health and needed her rest, as she is going on a long trip tomorrow. The fellow slipped into bed beside the woman, and she never moved. It looked kind of funny, but he was mighty careful not to touch her, because the lamp was a-burning and them men still set there a-playing cards. Pretty soon he went to sleep.

When he woke up the lamp had went out, and so was the fire. It was just a-getting light outdoors, and he could see that the gamblers was all gone. There wasn't nobody in the house but him and the woman. So he reached out to slip his arm around her, but she was cold as a stone. There was a big bullet-hole in her head, and it looked like she had been dead two or three days, anyhow.

The traveler got up and put his clothes on right quick, and

he run down the road fast as he could. The first town he come to, he told the sheriff what happened, and a bunch of men took him out there a-horseback. But when they got down and went in, the house was plumb empty. There wasn't no bed in it, and everything looked like nobody hadn't been there for a long time.

The sheriff and his deputies looked at the traveler kind of funny, but they didn't say much. When they got back to town the traveler just kept on a-traveling. He didn't go back there no more, neither. And so he never did find out where them gamblers come from, or who the woman was he slept with that night.

A Tall Fellow's Turkey

ONE TIME there was a little man lived away up on Gander Mountain. Times was awful hard, and there wasn't a bite of victuals in the house. But he had a pair of fine boots, so he put 'em on and come down to the main-traveled road. The little man figured on walking into town, because maybe he could sell the boots, or get something on credit at the store.

Pretty soon here come a big tall fellow carryin' a basket of groceries, and he had a nice turkey throwed over his shoulder. The little man seen him a-coming, so he pulled off one boot and dropped it in the road. And then he hid in the brush to see what happened.

The big tall fellow looked at the boot, and he says to himself, "Ain't that a dandy?" He thought some damn fools must have lost it out of their wagon. He felt of the leather and figured a pair of boots like that would cost a lot of money, what with prices like they are now. But one boot ain't no good to nobody, so the big fellow just left it a-laying there and tramped on down the road.

Soon as he was out of sight the little man come out of the brush and put on his boot. Then he took a short cut through the woods and run pretty fast, so as to get ahead of the big fellow again. This time he throwed the other boot down in the road, and hid in the brush just like he done before.

When the big fellow come along he says, "Hell's fire, there's the mate to the fine boot I seen back yonder!" and he figured it must have fell out of the same wagon. So he hid the boot and the groceries and the turkey in some brush, and then he started back after the other boot. He says to himself, if a fellow had a pair like that he could shine them up a little and sell 'em for ten dollars easy, or maybe fifteen.

So he run all the way back to where he seen the first boot, but it wasn't there. The big fellow rummaged around awhile, but the boot was plumb gone. Finally he give up, and went back to the place where he left his plunder. But when he got there the other boot was gone too, and so was the basket of groceries and the nice turkey.

The big fellow couldn't make head nor tail of it at first, but after while he figured out how somebody had played him for a sucker. He was pretty goddam mad too, and went a-stormin' up and down the road all evening, but there wasn't nothing he could do about it.

71

Some Other Small Gut

ONE TIME there was a fellow named Jud Brannan lived up in the Horse Shoe Bend country, and he was tryin' to court Sally Perkins. Jud was a good boy and a hard worker, but he didn't have no mother-wit. He was terrible thick-headed, and bashful to boot. Everybody knowed in reason poor Jud wasn't a-making no headway with Sally Perkins.

Jud asked his maw what was the best thing to do when you're a-courtin', and she told him to scrooch right up close and say, "Sal, you've stole my heart." Jud studied over it awhile, but he couldn't see no sense in such talk as that. "What else had I orter say, Maw?" The old woman just grinned. "You don't need to worry about nothin' else, son," she says. "Just keep on a-scroochin'. Sally Perkins an' old Mother Nature will take care of the rest."

Jud still couldn't see no sense in it, but he figured his maw knowed best. So all evenin' he kept sayin' to himself, "You've stole my heart, you've stole my heart, you've stole my heart," so he wouldn't forget what to tell Sally. He done fine until milkin' time, when the cow stepped on Paw's foot. "Soo thar," old man Brannan yelled, "before I kick the paunch out'n you!" And that's what broke the charm and throwed poor Jud off the track.

After supper Jud washed his feet and put on his boots. Then he slicked back his hair with possum grease and headed down to the Perkinses' place. Him and Sally set on a bench, and Jud scrooched up so close he could feel her a-breathin' and smell the new on her calico dress.

"Sal," says he, "you've done stole my paunch!"

Sally Perkins like to bust out laughing when she heard that, but Jud kept a-scrooching up to her, and she just drawed a long breath. "I reckon you mean I've stole your heart, Jud," she says kind of gentle-like.

Jud he begun to giggle. "Ain't it a sight, how some folks can remember things?" says he. "I knowed it was either that or some other small gut!"

This time Sally did bust out a-laughing sure enough. Jud giggled like a natural-born fool, but he kept a-scroochin' up to Sally just the same. And so everything worked out all right, just like Maw Brannan said it would.

Big Knives in Arkansas

ONE TIME a traveler from up North somewhere went down the other side of Blue Eye, and he stayed all night at a settlement way out in the woods. Along in the night he heard a lot of fiddling and hollering and stomping, because some of the neighbors was having a dance. The Yankee went over there. He hadn't never been to a square dance before, and he wanted to see how they do things in Arkansas.

The dance was in a log cabin with a puncheon floor. The folks was all good people, but they looked kind of tough to a city fellow. The young men wore their hair pretty long, and they danced Arkansas style with their hats on. Some of 'em hollered a little now and then, just to show they was having a good time. All them boys had big bowie knives in their belts, and the stranger was worried because he had never been around people like that before. The folks up in Missouri told him a lot of windy stories about how it was dangerous to travel in Arkansas, because the Arkansawyers are always a-feuding, and would kill each other any minute and think nothing of it.

When the set was over the boys led the girls over where they could set down on a bench, and then they all bowed very polite. But a minute later every man stepped back and pulled out his big long bowie knife. The city fellow thought there was going to be a terrible fight, so he broke right through the crowd. Everybody stared at him kind of surprised, but nobody said anything. The poor Yankee run into a corner far as he could and shut his eyes.

But he didn't hear nothing out of the ordinary, and when he

looked around the young men was all down on their knees, in front of the bench where the girls was a-setting. They didn't do no fighting at all, and there wasn't nothing to be afraid of. The Arkansas boys was all very quiet and peaceable. They just used them big knives to pick splinters out of the girls' feet.

Locusts Got the Corn

ONCE UPON A TIME there was a farmer that worked very hard. He plowed and harrowed and planted and hoed and pulled weeds, and raised a fine crop. So then he had bushels and bushels and bushels and bushels and bushels of corn. He got it all shucked, and put it in his big corn-crib, and thought how rich he was. But that was before the locusts come.

Finally a big locust found the farmer's corn, and he told all the other locusts for miles around. So the big locust come and got a grain of corn. Then another locust come and got another grain of corn. And another locust come and got another grain of corn. And another locust come and got another grain of corn. And another locust come and got another grain of corn. And another locust come and got another grain of corn. And another locust come and got another grain of corn. And another locust come and got another grain of corn. And another locust come and got another grain of corn. And another locust come . . .

The Time the Red Men Rode

ONE TIME there was a new lodge started up in town, and they called it the Red Men. A lot of the best citizens joined up, and they had a regular hall where they would go every Thursday night, and then lock the doors. Nobody could find out what they done in there, because it was a secret order same as the Masons and the Odd Fellows. The Red Men wouldn't let women in under no condition, and they didn't give no dances, neither.

Nothing happened till the Fourth of July, when all the country folks come to town. There was a fine big parade with pretty girls on hayracks, and folks carrying flags, and shooting off firecrackers, and the G.A.R. a-marching, and the Fife-and-Drum Corps, and the Knights of Pythias with swords, and fellows selling little balloons, and red lemonade in barrels, and popcorn balls, and a circle swing, and old Judge Lampson a-reading the Declaration, and a basket dinner in the courthouse yard, and things like that.

All of a sudden the folks heard a lot of shooting and hollering down by the livery barn. A fellow run out with blood all over his head, a-hollering "Indians! Indians!" And here they come, a-riding bareback with their ponies at a dead run. They was all stark naked only for a little britch-clout, and painted up something terrible, with feathers on besides. They was yelling loud as they could, and firing guns right into the crowd. The marshal shot back at 'em twice, and then he fell down in front of Tandy's drugstore and just laid there on the wooden sidewalk. Some folks' teams busted loose from the hichin'-rack, and there was runaways all over town, with several wagons turned over. Women was a-screaming and children a-crying and dogs a-barking. The old soldiers took out just like anybody else, and Captain Baker run into the butcher shop and hid under the counter. The whole business over in about two minutes, but there sure was hell to pay while it lasted. There ain't no use denying that everybody in town was scared plumb witless.

Pretty soon folks kind of come to their senses, and they seen them riders wasn't Indians at all. It was just the goddam Red Men fixed up like Indians, to scare everybody out of a year's growth. The marshal wasn't hurt a bit, because they was shooting blank cartridges without no bullets, and he was in cahoots with the Red Men all the time. So then folks begun to crawl out from wherever they was hid. Mostly they just grinned kind of sheepish, but some of the old soldiers was pretty mad.

If anybody was to play such a trick now, the people would know it was a put-up job. But things was different then. The Indian troubles was only a few years back, and not many miles off, neither. There was plenty of middle-aged men in town that had fought the Comanches. They'd seen folks buried with a cloth over their head, to hide where the scalps was gone. A fellow don't forget things like that in a hurry. Indians with war paint on 'em was took plumb serious in them days.

Job Was Pretty Stingy

ONE TIME there was a farmer named Job Perkins, and he saved every nickel he could get his hands on. He had a fine big house and lots of money, but he didn't have no fun, and neither did his wife. Folks used to say Job was so stingy he wouldn't go to the privy, for fear he might lose something. He figured that the longer a mess of victuals stayed in his innards, the more good they done him.

There was a fellow name of Jack lived down the road, and he had been tryin' to get the best of Job for a long time. Finally he come to the house with a empty bottle and says, "Job, I want to buy a quart of that applejack you got in your cellar." It is too bad, says Job, but the keg's never been tapped, and there ain't a spigot in the house. So Jack says he has got a brand-new spigot in his pocket, and he will pay two dollars, and Job can have the spigot for nothing. Two dollars is a lot of money for a quart of applejack, and Job figured the spigot was worth fifty cents besides, so he says all right.

Job tapped the keg and filled the bottle, but Jack had fixed the spigot so it couldn't be shut off nohow. The applejack dribbled right out on the floor, and Job had to stick his thumb in the hole to stop the leak. So Jack says you just wait till I fetch a big kettle to ketch the stuff in, and out of the cellar he run.

When Jack got to the kitchen Job's wife was glad to get a snort out of his bottle, and she says Job never lets her have a drink because applejack is worth money. Her and Jack drunk the whole bottle, and then they went in the other room and had more fun than you could shake a stick at. All this time they could hear Job yelling down in the cellar, but they knowed he wouldn't pull his thumb out of the spigot. Job couldn't stand to lose a whole keg of applejack, no matter what happened. Jack says this is the most fun he had since the hogs et up his brother, and Job's wife says it is the best time I ever did have all my life.

After Jack was gone she kind of straightened up the house, and then she went to the cellar and says, "Job, what on earth are you a-doing?" Job was so wore out he couldn't holler no more, but he still had his thumb stuck in the spigot. "Get me the big kettle," says he, and so she done it. And then he says, "Where's that goddam Jack?" She told him Jack come out with his bottle and rode off a long time ago. "Did he give you the two dollars?" says Job. "What for would he give me two dollars?" she says.

Job Perkins was a fellow that wouldn't never admit anybody has got the best of him. He went in the other room and looked round mighty careful, but it was all straightened up and he couldn't find nothing out of the way. So he just scowled at the old woman and never said no more about it.

A Pretty Girl in the Road

ONE TIME there was a fellow a-riding along and it was getting dark and coming on to rain besides. He seen a girl a-standing beside the road, where a old house had burnt down but the chimney was still there. She was a tall slim girl with a poke bonnet on, but he seen her face plain. He stopped and says if you are going somewheres I will give you a ride, because my horse carries double. She says her name is Stapleton, and her folks live down the road a piece. So then she jumped up behind him light as a feather. Pretty soon he spurred the horse a little, so she had to put her arms round his waist.

They rode on about a mile and he found out her first name was Lucy, and she wasn't married neither. He could feel her breath on his neck while they was a-talking, and he liked it fine. He got to thinking this was the kind of a girl he'd like to marry up with, because he liked her better than any girl he ever seen before.

So they rode another mile and it was pretty dark by this time, and they come to a graveyard. And there was a big house with lights in the windows just a little way off. She says that's where my folks live, but I'd better get down here. He figured she was going to take a short cut home, so her paw wouldn't know she had been riding with a stranger. Folks was awful particular about what their daughters done in them days. The girl jumped off and walked over to the gate. He says, "I'll be seein' you pretty soon," but Lucy just waved him goodbye and went into the graveyard.

The fellow waited awhile so she would have time to get home, and then he rode up in front of the big house. Soon as the dogs begun to bark an old man come out, and he says, "My name is Stapleton." He says the fellow is welcome to have supper with them and stay all night, as they have got plenty of room. And then he hollered a boy out of the barn to take care of the traveler's horse.

They had a mighty good supper, but there wasn't nobody at the table only Judge Stapleton and his wife. The fellow kept looking for Lucy to show up any minute, but she never come. So after while he went to bed in the spare room. It was a fine shuck mattress too, but he didn't sleep very good.

Next morning after breakfast they got to talking, and the Judge says him and his wife just moved here a year ago. "We used to live two miles down the road," he says, "but our house was lightnin'-struck and burnt plumb down. There ain't nothing left now but the old chimney." The fellow says yes, he seen that chimney when he rode by there last night. "I didn't mind losing the house," says the Judge, "only our daughter was sick in bed. We carried her out to the gate, but the shock was too much for her, and she died that same night."

The fellow just set there, and the Judge went on a-talkin' about what a fine girl his daughter was, and how him and the old woman was pretty lonesome nowadays. "We buried her in that little graveyard," says the Judge. "You can see her stone from the front gallery. There ain't a day goes by, rain or shine, that my wife don't walk over there an' set by the grave awhile."

Everything was mighty still for a minute, and then the traveler says, "What was your daughter's name?" It sounded kind of funny, the way he said it, but he was obliged to know.

"Her name was Lucy," says the Judge.

Groundhog Charley

ONE TIME there was a fellow lived out south of town, and he was kind of old-fashioned. He wore his beard and mustache long, and his hair hung plumb down to his shoulders. He kind of favored a summer groundhog, like some of them long-haired fellows they got in the movies nowadays, so everybody called him Groundhog Charley. After the tourists got to coming down here they was always taking pictures of him, to show the folks back home.

A bunch of them people was buying him drinks one day, and Charley told 'em a lot of big lies about how he used to fight Indians and all like that. Everybody was having a good time, but Groundhog Charley got pretty drunk. He begun to talk about killing somebody before sundown, so the marshal took his gun away. After while he pulled a big knife out of his boot, so then the marshal had to take the knife off him. Groundhog kept a-mumbling about how he aimed to wade knee-deep in blood, and maybe set the hotel afire besides. Finally the marshal got mad, and he started to put Groundhog Charley in the jailhouse.

He'd have done it too, sure as God made little apples, but some of Charley's friends promised they would take care of him. The marshal says all right, but be sure you keep the damn fool off the street, because we ain't running no Wild West show here. Charley went to sleep in the livery barn, and the boys thought they would play a joke on him. So they give him a clean shave and clipped his hair off right close to his head. Groundhog Charley woke up in the night and he felt mighty funny, but he couldn't make out what was the matter. Pretty soon he started for home, and some of the boys went along, to see that nothing didn't happen to him.

The house was all dark, and the boys helped Charley take off his boots on the front porch. They all waited around outside while he opened the door easy and got in bed with his wife. Groundhog didn't make a sound, but she run her hand over his head and face. "Stranger," she says, "I don't know who you are, or how come you in this house. But if there's anything here you want, you better take it quick. My old man's liable to come home any minute!"

Of course, the chances are Groundhog Charley's wife never said nothing like that at all, and the whole thing is just a made-up tale. But them boys all swore it was true as God's own gospel, and they told the story around this town for more than twenty-five years.

The King's Daughter Laughed

ONE TIME there was a king had a pretty daughter, but she was kind of sad all the time. She looked healthy, and the doctors couldn't find nothing wrong with her. Everybody says she must be witched, or maybe hippoed. She just set there all day mute as a mouse, and never said one word only if the king asked her a question. Nobody seen her smile in seven years, and some folks thought maybe she was losing her mind. So finally the old king says that if any man makes the girl laugh he can marry her, and get a big farm besides, and gold to go with it.

There was young fellows come from all over the country, a-trying to make the king's daughter laugh. They sung songs and told stories and danced jigs and turned summersets and done all kind of tricks. But the king's daughter just watched them awhile, and then she would look out of the window. Some of them boys fetched in clowns, and trained animals, and fireworks, and all kind of things like that. But it didn't do no good. The king's daughter never laughed once.

There was a big farm boy come along one day, and he had a pig that could stand on its hind legs and dance. The farm boy had brought some fancy clothes in a poke and a tin whistle he was going to blow while the pig was a-dancing. Some smart-alecks put the farm boy in a little closet to change his clothes, and they fed the pig a whole churnful of buttermilk. Then one of them put some turpentine under the pig's tail.

The next thing anybody knowed, here come the pig right through the house, a-squealing fit to wake the dead, with buttermilk a-squirting out behind. And here come the big farm boy stark naked, with the tin whistle in his hand, hollering "Soo-ey! Soo-ey!" at the top of his voice.

The king's daughter just took one look, with her mouth open and her eyes a-sticking out like doorknobs. Then she busted out a-laughing, and you could hear it all over the place, with the pig still a-squealing and the farm boy hollering "Soo-ey! Soo-ey!" The king's servants run in by this time and chased the pig out, and they hustled the farm boy back into the closet where his clothes was at. Pretty soon here come the old king himself to see what was going on, but his daughter was still a-laughing so hard she couldn't tell him nothing.

Some of the servants was fixing to put the farm boy in jail, because they figured he has insulted the quality folks. But the king's daughter just laughed, and the old king stood there a-looking at her kind of thoughtful. Pretty soon she stopped laughing, and she says have that young man put his clothes on and come in here, because I got something to tell him.

After while the big farm boy come in and he started a-talking how the whole thing was a accident, because them smart-alecks turpentined his pig while he was changing clothes. The king's daughter says never mind the pig, the thing is do you want to marry me? And the farm boy says, "Yes, ma'am." The king's daughter says that's fine, because you are the only man in this country I would even think about marrying. The old king he just looked at both of them for a minute, and then they all laughed like fools. And so the big farm boy married the king's daughter, and they lived happy ever after.

Boots on the Wire

ONE TIME there was an old-time farmer that didn't know nothing about machinery. When they built the railroad across his farm the old man used to come down every day to see the train go through, like it was kind of a miracle. He thought the telegraph wire had something to do with running the train, but it was a long time before they could get him to believe that you could send a message on it.

85

Well, the farmer's boy was a-living in town, and the young fellow wanted his boots. So the old man cleaned the boots up and greased them right good, and then he got ready to drive into town. But a smart-aleck come along and says anybody is a fool to drive all that way in a wagon, because it is thirty miles and a fellow would be on the road all day. And then it will take another day to get back home, too.

The old farmer says yes, that's so, but my boy has got a dress-up job in town, and he needs these here boots right away. The smart-aleck says all you got to do is write the boy's name on a piece of paper and put it in the boots, and then hang the boots on the telegraph wire. They will go through same as a telegram, he says, and your boy can get 'em the first thing in the morning, and it will only cost ten cents. The old man says it's a damn good idea, and a lot easier than to drive sixty miles in a wagon, with the creek a-rising besides.

So then they went up to the house and drunk some cider, and the farmer says, "You write my boy's name on this here paper, because I cain't see to write without my specs." The smart-aleck wrote the name on the paper, and then he rode off towards the river. Just before dark he sneaked back through the woods, and sure enough there was a fine pair of boots hanging on the wire. The smart-aleck stole them boots and went on down the road.

Next morning the old farmer seen the boots was gone, so he figured everything was all right. But when the boy come back home next month he says he never got the boots. The old man says, "I don't see how that could be, as I sure sent 'em to you." When the boy found out what happened, he says, "God damn it, that feller slickered you out of my good boots!"

The old man thought a long time, and finally he figured it

86

out. "That smart-aleck must have knowed I cain't read writin'," says he. "I bet the son-of-a-bitch wrote somebody else's name on that paper! And then his partner went to the telegraph office and paid the ten cents, so naturally they give him your boots!"

The boy looked at the old man a minute, and he swallered a couple of times, and then he drawed a deep breath.

"I reckon you're right, Paw," says he. "I reckon that must be how they done it."

The Magic Horn

ONE TIME there was a fellow the boys used to call Pokeroot, and he owned a nice farm. But the rich banker cheated him out of it some way. So Pokeroot and his wife had to give up their good house and live in a little shanty. They pretty near froze the first winter and couldn't get no meat only rabbits. Every night Pokeroot and his wife would set in the shanty and talk how they would like to fix the rich banker that cheated them out of their nice farm.

Pokeroot's wife was part Indian, and she could make red dye out of weeds. They got a hog's bladder and filled it up with this red stuff, and she put the bladder inside the front of her dress. Next time the rich banker come along, Pokeroot and his wife begun to fight each other, and all of a sudden he stuck a knife in her belly. The red dye come a-pouring out just like blood, and Mistress Pokeroot fell down and laid there with her mouth open.

The rich banker turned white as a toadstool and started to run off, but Pokeroot just laughed. "She's dead all right," says he, "but it don't make no difference. I got something that will fetch her back to life." He had a little old tooter made out of a cow's horn, with some Indian signs carved on it. "Just watch me," says Pokeroot. And he stuck the horn under his wife's petticoat and blowed loud and shrill. She jumped up a-laughing and danced round as lively as ever. Pokeroot told the rich banker it's a magic horn he got from the Choctaws, and it will raise a dead person every time. All you got to do is stick it up under their petticoat.

The rich banker got to thinking how lots of people might pay big money for a charm like that, and he wanted to buy the horn right now, but Pokeroot wouldn't sell it. After while the rich banker pulled out seven ten-dollar gold pieces and throwed 'em down on the table, so Pokeroot give him the magic horn. The banker got on his horse and high-tailed it for home, with the little tooter stuck in his belt. He looked like he was mighty pleased. Pokeroot and his wife laughed about it all evening.

Next day Pokeroot went to town and the folks was all worked up about something, so he says, "What is the matter?" And they told him how the rich banker has stabbed his housekeeper with a butcher knife. And when the sheriff got there he seen the woman laying dead on the floor, with blood all over the place. The rich banker was a-blowing up under her dress with a cow's horn, a-jabbering how he would fetch her back to life. Everybody knowed he was trying to play crazy and fool the people so they wouldn't hang him. It didn't do no good, though. The jury says the rich banker was guilty in the first degree, and the judge sent him off to the penitentiary. And everybody says it served the son-of-a-bitch right.

There Was an Old Woman

ONE TIME there was a smart fellow come from up North somewhere, and he was always making fun of us country folks. He knowed a lot of jokes and wisecracks that we never heard tell of, and he made it look like the people that lived out our way didn't have no sense. He wasn't no sissy, neither. When a long-haired boy from Hardtail Mountain jumped onto him, the smart fellow dodged them haymakers easy. And then he just stepped in close for one little tap on the jaw. It looked like his fist didn't move more'n four inches, but the Hardtail Mountain boy was knocked plumb senseless, and he didn't come to for a long time. Ab Stockstill pulled a knife on him one evening, but the Yankee kicked it out of his hand and beat poor Ab till he bellered like a calf.

The home boys got so they would sing a little song every time the smart fellow come along, and it went like this:

> There was an old woman an' she could do,
> She could do, she could do,
> There was an old woman an' she could do,
> She could do, she could do.

Whenever he would pass anybody on the road, or plowing in the field, or running a sorghum mill, they was always a-singing about the old woman an' she could do. When he went in the tavern the boys would sing about the old woman so loud you couldn't hear the juke-box, and even the kids coming home from school got to singing the same thing. The Yankee figured there must be some kind of a catch to it, so he just let on like he never heard the song at all.

In the back of the poolhall one day the Southern Harmony Quartet had got together, and they was a-practicing for the big Fourth of July singing convention. They stood there a-looking in each other's eyes with their heads close together, and they was a-singing:

> There was an old woman an' she could do,
> She could do, she could do,
> There was an old woman an' she could do,
> She could do, she could do.

All of a sudden the Yankee couldn't stand it no longer. "For God's sake," he says, "what could she do?" The boys in the quartet just rolled their eyes at him, solemn as owls, and then they sung the next verse:

> She could go to hell an' so can you,
> So can you, so can you,
> She could go to hell an' so can you,
> So can you, so can you.

Jim Blevins is the best bass singer in the whole country, and when he dropped down about two octaves on the last "so can you" folks clear out in the street could hear the window glass a-rattling. They let the quartet sing it through once, and then everybody joined in. There was some people kept a-hollering "Amen!" like it was a regular camp meeting.

The smart fellow seen they was all laughing at him, so he marched out of the poolhall. But everybody was in on it, and after that whenever he passed anybody on the road they would be singing about how the old woman could go to hell and so can you. The kids coming home from school all sung the same

90

thing, and so did the girls that worked in the hotel. And even if some boy was plowing way out in the country, he would begin to sing whenever the smart fellow come along the road.

Things went on like that every day, but the smart Yankee didn't say a word. Finally one night he went to a dinner the Methodist ladies was giving. It only cost twenty-five cents for all the chicken you could eat, and a lot of other stuff besides. Just about time he finished his pie, a girl begun to play the "old woman" tune on the church organ.

When he heard that tune right in the church house, the Yankee seen he was beat. He just grinned a little and waved everybody goodbye. Then he got his suitcase at the hotel and caught the rattler out of town. That was the last anybody ever seen of him. The folks figured he must have went back up North somewheres.

The Toadfrog

ONE TIME there was a pretty girl walking down the street, and she heard somebody say, "Hi, Toots!" But when she looked around there was nobody in sight, just a little old toadfrog setting on the sidewalk.

So then the pretty girl started to walk on down the street, and she heard somebody say, "Hello, Beautiful!" But when she looked around there was nobody in sight, just this little old toadfrog.

So then the pretty girl started to walk on down the street,

and she heard somebody say, "You got anything on tonight, Baby?" But when she looked around there was nobody in sight, just this little old toadfrog setting on the sidewalk.

The pretty girl looked down at the little old toadfrog. "I know it ain't you a-talking," she says.

"It's me, all right," says the toadfrog. "I'm a handsome young man, by rights. But I'm turned into a toadfrog now, because an old witch put a spell on me."

The pretty girl studied awhile, and then she says, "Ain't there anything you can do to break the spell?"

The toadfrog says there is only one way, and that is for a pretty girl to let him sleep on her pillow all night. The pretty girl thought it was the least she could do, to help this poor fellow out. So she took the little old toadfrog home and put him on her pillow when she went to bed.

Next morning the pretty girl's father come to wake her up, and he seen a handsome young man in the bed with her. She told her father about the little old toadfrog, and the witch that put a spell on him, and how it all happened. But the old man didn't believe the story, any more than you do!

Old Black-Oak Knows Best

ONE TIME there was a pretty girl named Josie, and her folks was well fixed but they had trouble with the law, so the town boys didn't come around much. There was a young farmer name of Pete wanted to go with her, but Josie wouldn't do it because she figured them high-collar town boys was better. She give old Gram French two dollars for a charm, but it didn't do no good. Finally Gram told her to hang the charm on the old black-oak at midnight, and then say a little rhyme.

When Josie come to the old black-oak she done just like Gram told her, and then set down to see what happened. Pretty soon she heard a voice away up in the air a-mumbling. Josie was kind of scared, but she stood still a minute and listened. There was some more mumbling, and then the voice says, "You got to marry Pete." Josie run for home when she heard that and never told the folks nothing.

The next night she went back to the old black-oak and done just like Gram told her, and then set down to see what happened. Pretty soon she hears some more mumbling up in the air, and then the voice says, "You got to marry Pete." Josie went home and thought about it a long time.

The third night she went back to the old black-oak and done just like Gram told her, and then set down to see what happened. Pretty soon she heard something a-mumbling up in the air, and then the voice says, "You got to marry Pete." Josie went home just like she done before, and never slept a wink all night.

Next day she went and told Gram French what happened. "If you heerd the same thing three nights a-runnin', you better go ahead an' marry Pete," says Gram. "What's the use to marry a fellow like that?" says Josie. "Why, he ain't got a pot to cook in, or a window to throw it out!" Gram just set and looked at her awhile. "Old black-oak knows best," she says. "It takes more'n pots an' windows to make a good husband." Gram didn't say no more, and Josie didn't return no answer.

Josie told the folks she knowed all the time it was Pete

a-talking out of the old black-oak, and she says Gram French must have put him up to it. But Pete just grinned, and he never did admit nothing. Him and her got hitched in the dark of the moon, all right. But the neighbors say they done about as good as any other married folks.

The Good Girl and the Ornery Girl

ONE TIME there was an old woman lived away out in the timber, and she had two daughters. One of them was a good girl and the other one was ornery, but the old woman liked the ornery one best. So they made the good girl do all the work, and she had to split wood with a dull axe. The ornery girl just laid a-flat of her back all day and never done nothing.

The good girl went out to pick up sticks, and pretty soon she seen a cow. The cow says, "For God's sake milk me, my bag's about to bust!" So the good girl milked the cow, but she didn't drink none of the milk. Pretty soon she seen a apple tree, and the tree says, "For God's sake pick these apples, or I'll break plumb down!" So the good girl picked the apples, but she didn't eat none. Pretty soon she seen some cornbread a-baking, and the bread says, "For God's sake take me out, I'm a-burning up!" So the good girl pulled the bread out, but she didn't taste a crumb. A little old man come along just then, and he throwed a sack of gold money so it stuck all over her. When the good girl got home she shed gold pieces like feathers off a goose.

Next day the ornery girl went out to get her some gold too. Pretty soon she seen a cow, and the cow says, "For God's sake milk me, my bag's about to bust!" But the ornery girl just kicked the old cow in the belly, and went right on. Pretty soon she seen a apple tree, and the tree says, "For God's sake pick these apples, or I'll break plumb down!" But the ornery girl just laughed, and went right on. Pretty soon she seen some corn-bread a-baking, and the bread says, "For God's sake take me out, I'm a-burning up!" But the ornery girl didn't pay no mind, and went right on. A little old man come along just then, and he throwed a kettle of tar so it stuck all over her. When the ornery girl got home she was so black the old woman didn't know who it was.

The folks tried everything they could, and finally they got most of the tar off. But the ornery girl always looked kind of ugly after that, and she never done any good. It served the little bitch right, too.

Mister Fox

ONE TIME there was some people lived up the creek, and they had a pretty daughter named Elsie. She never went with the boys much till a stranger come along all dressed up, and he took her to the dances. Elsie had a good time, and she believed everything he said. She thought Mister Fox hung the moon. After while the stranger told her to get all the money and jewelry she could and meet him down by the crossroads Friday midnight. He says he will come with two horses, and they will run off and get married. So Elsie says all right.

When Elsie got there it wasn't midnight yet, so she climbed up in a tree just for a joke. Pretty soon here come Mister Fox and two other fellows. They looked all round but they did not see her, so they begun to dig a hole in the ground. She could hear them talking about how they would take some girl's money and jewelry and fine clothes. And then Mister Fox was going to kill the girl, so that was why they dug the big hole to bury her in. Elsie knowed then that Mister Fox was nothing but a robber. Him and them other fellows just went around the country a-killing people and stealing their stuff.

The robbers waited a long time, and Elsie just laid quiet on a big limb. Finally Mister Fox says, "That fool girl must have forgot what day it is, because she ain't got the sense God give a goose. But never mind, we will get her some other night," says he. So then him and the other robbers covered the hole up with some brush and rode back to town.

After while Elsie slipped down the tree and walked home through the woods. She told her folks what happened. The boys wanted to go and kill Fox right away, but the old man says no, we will take our time and ketch the whole gang. So they called the kinfolks to come over to a big dance. Elsie sent word for Mister Fox to come and bring his friends, because they had more girls for the dance than there was boys.

After they danced a few sets the folks all set down to drink cider and eat cake. One fellow sung a couple of songs, and then they got to telling riddles. When it come Elsie's turn she says:

> Riddle-dum riddle-dum rideo,
> What did I see last Friday-o,

96

The wind blew high, my heart did ache
To see the hole a fox did make.

When Mister Fox heard that he knowed Elsie had found out something. He got up right easy and reached under his coat, but Elsie's pappy let fire with the shotgun and pretty near cut him in two. The boys jumped on them other robbers, and killed both of 'em right now. Then they hauled the three corpses down to the crossroads. Them robbers was carrying silver-mounted pistols, and they had rings on their fingers, and their pockets full of gold besides. The folks took all this stuff, and then throwed the corpses into the grave they dug for Elsie.

After that poor Elsie wouldn't go with nobody, because she figured men was all son-of-a-bitches. And so she never did get married at all, but just stayed around with the kinfolks. They was glad to have her, of course. But it is kind of sad to see a pretty girl bound and determined to be an old maid like that.

The Bull Was Found Guilty

ONE TIME there was a farmer had a nice little cornpatch under rail, and there was a bull come along and ruined it. That bull was the breachiest critter that ever lived, and he could bust through a stake-an'-rider fence like a mess of spider webs. When the farmer seen the shape his corn was in, he told the Justice of the Peace. The constable went out after the man that owned the bull, but the man was not home. So the constable arrested the breachy bull, and come a-leading the critter into the settlement.

There was some jackleg lawyers around town, and they says it ain't legal to try a bull no matter what he done. But the Squire didn't pay no attention, and they had the trial under a big oak tree. A big crowd come to see it, and some of the boys was pretty drunk. The bull bellered and pawed up dust, so the constable couldn't keep no order. The lawyers argued pretty near all day. One lawyer says the Squire is the damndest fool he ever seen, but they fined him two dollars for contempt of court. Finally the Squire decided the bull is guilty of trespass and destroying valuable property, so the critter must pay twenty-five dollars and costs.

The constable says the bull ain't got no money, and what will we do now? The Squire thought about it awhile, and then he says, "Butcher the varmint, an' sell the meat!" So that's what they done. It wasn't no time till people was building fires and cooking beef all over the place. Everybody got their chin greasy, but the Squire took the hide and tallow. The folks all sung songs and chawed fat and guggled whiskey out of the same jug. Before sundown the Squire and the lawyers was drunk as anybody. The whole lot of 'em was a-dancing round the fire and yelling like Indians.

Next morning everybody seen they had made a fool out of theirself, and the least said the soonest mended. Some of the old-timers says the whole thing is a joke, and it never really happened at all. And even if something peculiar did happen, there ain't no way to find out who was to blame. So then some of the boys took up a collection for the fellow that owned the bull, and never said no more about it.

When Lizzie Picked the Greens

ONE TIME there was a killing up on Pucketts Run, and the sheriff come out to see about it. He was talking to a bonehead family name of Taylor, that had seven grown boys and five big girls. They all just stood around with their mouth open, mostly. But the Taylors lived right by the ford, so the sheriff thought he better ask 'em some questions anyhow.

"Did you see anybody cross the creek this morning?" he says to a big gal named Lizzie. "No, I was pickin' a mess of greens," she says, a-giggling kind of foolish. Then he asked one of the big boys. "I didn't see nobody," says the boy, " 'cause I wasn't home. I been down to the Blue Hole a-fishin'." The sheriff looked at him mighty sharp. "John," says he, "what time did you get back?" John studied awhile, and then he says, "Just before Lizzie picked the greens."

The sheriff turned his back on John and tackled another boy. "Bill," he says, "when did John come in?" Bill scratched his head and studied awhile. "Near as I can recollect, it was while I was a-milkin'," says he. "Well, what time did you do the milking?" the sheriff asked. "Right after breakfast, same as always," Bill told him. The whole family was a-giggling, but the sheriff never paid no mind. "Did you have breakfast early, Mis' Taylor?" he says. The old woman looked pretty sour. "No, we didn't," says she. "Why not?" says the sheriff. "Couldn't split no wood, till Tom got back with the axe. Them

99

coon hunters is all alike," she says. "Tom," says the sheriff, "when did you get home?" Tom he studied awhile, and then his face lit up like he remembered something all of a sudden. "Just about the time Lizzie picked the greens, sheriff," says he.

The sheriff was a-cussing under his breath by now, but pretty soon he says, "Lizzie, this is a serious business. I got to know when you picked them goddam greens. Was it six o'clock? Or seven? Or do you reckon it was nearer to eight?"

Lizzie giggled, and looked at the sheriff sideways. "I been

thinkin' about that," she says. "We didn't eat no greens this mornin', an' there ain't no greens in the house now. I reckon it must have been *last* week I picked the greens!"

Nobody said another word, and the sheriff just stood there with his mouth open like the rest of them. And then he got in his buggy and drove off. The boys say he was a-talking to himself all the way back to town.

The Boy and the Turkeys

ONE TIME there was a boy hid in a corn-crib, and he was laying for some wild turkeys that come there to eat the corn. When the turkeys showed up, the boy give a jump right into the middle of the flock and grabbed two of them big gobblers. But the gobblers was stronger than he figured, and they flew off with him hanging onto their legs. The next thing that boy knowed he was way up in the air, looking down at the treetops.

The boy sure was in a bad fix, but pretty soon he figured out what was the best thing to do. He turned one of them turkeys loose and held onto the other one. The old gobbler flopped his wings like a windmill, but he couldn't quite make it. So down they come, slow and easy. Soon as his feet touched the ground the boy wrung the turkey's neck and started for home.

It was way after dark when he got to the house, because them turkeys had carried him fourteen miles while he was figuring out what to do. The folks didn't believe the story at first, and they was going to give him a licking for lying. But

101

when he showed 'em the big old gobbler, they just didn't know what to think.

Finally the old man says maybe that fool boy is telling the truth, because nobody in this family has got sense enough to make up such a lie out of his own head. And besides, how could he ketch a big wild turkey like that, without a mark on it only its neck broke?

The folks didn't say much about the turkey story for a week or two, but after while they got so they would tell it for the gospel truth. And finally the old man told a preacher that he looked out the window just as the two turkeys was carryin' the boy over the treetops. "I never would have believed such a tale," says he, "if I hadn't seen it with my own eyes!"

Arithmetic on Bear Creek

ONE TIME there was a fellow got drunk pretty near every day, and he generally come home away late in the night. So naturally his wife got kind of lonesome, and the neighbor's hired man used to come over to see her. The hired man's name was Oliver.

Well, one night Oliver and the drunk man's wife was at home the same as usual, and they heard somebody a-stumbling around outside. Oliver knowed it was the woman's husband, and he started to jump out of bed. But the woman says, "Stay right where you're at. He's so drunk he won't never notice." So Oliver just laid there.

When the drunk man come in he didn't light no candle. He

just undressed in the dark, quiet as he could. You could hear the things in his pockets rattle when he dropped the overalls on the floor. Then the drunk man crawled in next to his wife. The moonlight come in over the end of the bed, and the drunk man kept a-looking down there like he seen something that bothered him. "Mary," says he, "there's too many feet in this bed!" and then he counted out loud, "One, two, three, four, five, six."

The woman says, "No such a thing, John. It just looks that way, because you've been a-drinkin'. Go to sleep, an' everything will be all right in the mornin'." But the drunk man kept on a-counting them feet, and it come out six every time. "There's somethin' mighty funny here," says he, "an' I better see about it."

He got up and stumbled round to the foot of the bed, and then he begun to count, "One, two, three, four." And the woman says, "There's only four feet, John, like I told you. You got two, an' I got two. Two and two is four, ain't it?" The drunk man counted 'em again, "One, two, three, four." And then he says, "I guess you're right, Mary. But I would have swore there was six a minute ago."

So then he got back into bed and went to sleep, like his wife said.

Grind the Coffee

ONE TIME there was a bunch of girls wanted to play "Grind the Coffee," but they didn't have no jumping-rope. Good ropes wasn't common in them days, and

103

if a girl was to use the well-rope she'd get a licking soon as the folks found it out. So mostly they would cut a nice straight grapevine and play with that if there wasn't no rope handy.

While the girls was a-gabbling about how they didn't have no rope, here come a fellow name of Jerry Stillwell. He was a big good-looking boy and not very bright, so the girls all thought he was God's own cousin. Jerry says of course he will get 'em a jumping-rope, and glad to do it. Anything to convenience the ladies is my motto, he says. So away they went with all them girls a-hanging onto Jerry, like a flock of pullets after a young rooster.

By the time they got to the woods poor Jerry's head was spinning like a top. But pretty soon he seen a nice straight grapevine a-hanging down from a tall gum tree. Jerry clumb that vine like a squirrel, with a big knife between his teeth. When he got up about twenty feet the girls was all hollering about what a wonderful climber he was.

Jerry turned his head to look down at 'em, and he was grinning so they could see what fine white teeth he had. It looks like anybody would have knowed better, but poor Jerry was thinking about something else. So all of a sudden he reached up the old frog-sticker and cut the vine off over his head. Down came the whole business, and Jerry hit the ground KER-WHOOMP! The wind was knocked plumb out of him for a minute, so he just laid there with his mouth wide open.

The girls was all a-squealing like pigs at a cutting-match. Some of them run to the creek and fetched water, but mostly they was a-pullin' poor Jerry around to untangle him out of the grapevine. Soon as he ketched his breath, Jerry begun to holler so loud you could hear him plumb to the road. He says both legs is broke, and his backbone throwed out of joint besides. And he says don't pour no more water on me, because I am wet as a mushrat already. So finally they got a fellow to load Jerry on a wagon and haul him into town. Old Doc Holton looked him over mighty careful, and he says there ain't nothing much wrong with Jerry. Just bruised and skinned up, he says, but no bones broke. And when they told Doc how it happened, he laughed right in Jerry's face.

As soon as they found out Jerry wasn't hurt, the girls told everybody how he cut the vine off, and pretty soon people was laughing about it all over the country. Jerry Stillwell couldn't take a joke. For a long time after that he would fight anybody if they so much as mentioned grapevines, or jumping-ropes, or "Grind the Coffee."

The Magic Cowhide

ONE TIME there was a boy named Jack, and his folks died and left a good farm. But when they come to divide up it was his two older brothers that heired the farm, and Jack didn't get nothing but an old cow. Pretty soon the cow died, so Jack didn't have nothing, and then his brothers says he better go to town and get a job somewheres. Jack skinned the cow and started out to sell the hide, or else maybe he could trade it for something. Every house he come to he would ask the people, but they all says they don't want no stinking old cowhide.

When it come night Jack laid down on the ground, and he put the cowskin over him. Pretty soon he woke up and the sun was shining. There was a lot of crows on top of him, a-pecking away at the cowhide. Jack grabbed one of the crows and made a little cage for it out of willow switches. He thought maybe he could split the crow's tongue and learn it how to talk.

Pretty soon he heard somebody a-coming, so Jack hid in the brush and held the crow's bill shut. It was two robbers, and they was talking how they had buried a lot of gold under the fireplace in Sim Lawton's cabin while Sim was out a-working, so he didn't know nothing about it.

After the robbers was gone Jack walked on till he come to a house, and the man says his name is Sim Lawton. "Well," says Jack, "me and the crow was talking about you last night." Sim he just laughed. "The crow says there's gold buried on your place," says Jack, "an' I'll show you where it is, only you must give me half." Sim laughed louder than ever. "Take half an' welcome," he says, "but you two birds have got to do the diggin', because I won't turn my hand to no such foolishness." So then Jack prized up the hearthstone, and sure enough there was a big sack of gold pieces.

They split the gold even, but Sim says he will give half of his share for the crow, and Jack let him have it. Sim figured he would travel around with the crow and find out where folks has hid their money. So Jack walked on down the road, with three fourths of the robbers' gold wrapped up in his cowhide.

Jack stayed at the hotel all night, and next day here comes Sim, and he was pretty mad. "This fool crow won't talk," says he. "It just goes *quark, quark,* and so I want my money back." But Jack just laughed in his face. "The bird talks all right," he says, "but a man can't understand crow language till he sleeps three nights under the magic cowhide."

Sim wanted to borrow the cowhide for a few days, but Jack wouldn't hear of it. So finally Sim handed over the rest of the

106

robbers' gold, and Jack give him the stinkin' old cowhide. Jack had all the gold now, and he went to Little Rock. Sim Lawton took several trips down there to look for him, but Jack was plumb gone. Some say he went partners with them Hot Springs gamblers and got rich, but the folks never did find out for sure.

Stiff As a Poker

ONE TIME there was an old man, and some say his name was Benton. He was a heavy drinker, and one night he passed out, so his friends put him in the icehouse. Then they got to drinking, and forgot all about him. Two or three days later somebody happened to go in the icehouse, and there was the old man froze stiff as a poker. The boys felt awful bad about it, but they didn't know what to do. They jowered awhile, and then decided to thaw the body out and tell the folks he died of heart trouble or something. So they fetched the old man into the house and laid him on the bed.

Next day a woman went in to look at the corpse, and when she seen that old Benton was a-breathing she fainted plumb away. The folks sent for the doctor and put hot towels on him, and they poured some whiskey between his teeth. Pretty soon the old devil was setting up chipper as a jaybird. He says he feels better than he had in a long time. The old man didn't remember nothing about being froze in the icehouse, so the folks never told him. They figured he wouldn't believe it, anyhow.

They told the doctor what happened, though, and he just

107

laughed at 'em. The doctor says he seen catfish froze solid for two or three months and then thawed out alive, but he never heard tell of it being tried on a man. Old hunters claim that bears and groundhogs and chipmunks lay up all winter; maybe a man could do the same, if he set his mind to it. But everybody knowed that Doc was a-joking.

It was about a year after that when old man Benton got to drinking and raising hell worse than ever. One night him and his friends all got drunk, and the old man passed out. The first thing anybody knowed them damn fools put him in the icehouse again, and this time they let him freeze solid for more'n a month. Then they fetched him in the house, and he thawed out a-feelin' fine. One of the boys told him this time, but the old man just laughed, as he did not believe a word of it.

After that the folks used to freeze old man Benton every so often, and seemed like it agreed with him fine. A quick freeze and a slow thaw-out done the old devil good. Doc Holton come along one day, so the boys took him down to the icehouse and he seen old man Benton a-layin' there, froze hard as a rock. Doc says a joke is a joke, but this man's dead! You damn fools have killed him, and I will have to tell the sheriff about it. But the boys says just keep your shirt on, Doc, and watch us thaw him out. So they done just like always, and pretty soon old man Benton got to breathing again. He was pretty slow coming out of it this time, though. Doc set up with him all night, but the next morning old man Benton was dead sure enough.

"Well, boys," says Doc, "I never seen nothing like this before, and maybe I am going crazy. I don't know what this fellow died of, but there ain't no sign of frostbite. He was an old man anyhow, so I am going to put it down heart disease and try to forget the whole business. But from now on if you freeze

108

anybody else I will see that you go to the penitentiary, and I ain't joking neither." So then Doc got in his buggy and went back to town.

Everybody is mighty close-mouthed about them things nowadays, on account of the tourists and all. But the folks up that way are still a-putting up ice, and lots of 'em have got padlocks on their icehouses.

Casting Out the Devil

ONE TIME there was a preacher come a-riding up to a house. The man was away from home, but the woman had a young fellow in there, and the preacher seen him through the window. It was a little log cabin, and they didn't have but one door. The woman asked the preacher to come in, and he set down by the fire. Pretty soon he figured out that the young fellow must be hid in a barrel with some cotton rags on top, but he never let on.

The woman talked polite enough, and she says she's a Methodist, but her husband is a out-and-out infidel. She kind of hinted maybe the preacher better go away, because her man is kind of mean, particular if he's been a-drinking. But the preacher says he knows how to handle infidels, and he has brought hundreds of 'em to the repentance of their sinful ways. So he just set right where he was.

After while her man come home, and he was pretty drunk. He says right off that preachers don't do nothing nowadays only run after the womenfolks and eat yellow-leg chickens.

Why don't they heal the sick and raise the dead and cast out devils, he says, like the saints done back in Bible times?

The preacher just looked at the man a little bit, and then he says, "Is anybody sick in this house, that you want me to heal 'em?" The man says no. "Is anybody dead here, that you want me to raise 'em up?" So the man says no again. "Well," says the preacher, "there's a devil in the house, all right. Just watch me cast him out!" And with that he throwed a shovelful of live coals into the barrel.

Well, sir, them cotton rags blazed up just like gunpowder, and filled the house full of smoke. The young fellow in the barrel roared like a bull, and out he come with his clothes afire. Right through the door he went, a-trailing smoke and yelling at every jump. You could hear him a-hollering plumb to the creek, and then come a big splash. The infidel just set there with his mouth open. He was pretty drunk, and the room was full of smoke, so he thought maybe it was the devil sure enough. "Let's pray!" says the preacher, and there they was both down on their knees, with the unbeliever a-praying loud as anybody.

When the preacher says "Amen" they got up, and both of 'em was looking mighty solemn. After while the man says, "Parson, how did you know the devil was in that barrel?" The preacher just looked at him a minute. "I never seen a infidel's house yet, but what there was a devil in it," says he. "Sometimes there's two or three of 'em." And with that he told the folks goodbye and rode off down the trail.

The infidel stayed close to home for a long time after that, and he quit drinking, too. It looked for awhile like he was going to join the church, but he never done it. Him and his woman treated preachers mighty respectful though, and he didn't have nothing more to say about yellow-leg chickens.

The Burying of Old Man Kane

ONE TIME there was an old man named Kane, and he was a-dying. After Doc Holton give him up, the old man just laid there a-cussing. There was a preacher come around and wanted him to repent and join the church. But old man Kane says he's lived a infidel and he aims to die a infidel, and they can just let the tail go with the hide.

"I don't want no preachin' and prayin' after I'm dead, neither," says he. "If any snivellin' parson comes a-conjurin' round, he'll foller me into the grave!"

It's terrible bad luck for a dyin' man to talk to a fellow like that, and the preacher looked mighty uneasy. All of a sudden old man Kane started a-spewin' out blood, and pretty soon he was dead. The womenfolks kept a-pestering the parson to preach the funeral, but he wouldn't promise nothing. But after the boys got the grave dug it was a-raining, and that's a good sign. So finally the preacher give in. "It's ag'in my feeling to pray over a man that don't want to be prayed over," says he. "But I cain't stand here and see one of my neighbors throwed into his grave like a wild varmint, even if he wasn't a Christian."

The dirt was mighty soft all round where the boys had been digging, and wet. The preacher stood there at the head of the grave a-praying. Just a few words, and then he motioned the boys to let the coffin down. One end come loose from the ropes, and maybe spattered a little water. The preacher was pretty nervous, and he give a jump that throwed him off'n his bal-

111

ance. He let out a terrible whoop just as his feet slipped, and then he fell right slap-dab into the grave!

Soon as he ketched his breath the preacher tried to get out, but the edge of the hole was too slick, and he kept a-slipping back onto the coffin. Folks was a-milling around every which way, and falling down in the mud, and hollering out what to do about it. He sure was a sorry-looking parson when the boys finally drug him out. You wouldn't have knowed him scarcely, he was so gaumed up and bedobbled.

"Oh God!" says he. "I *did* foller him into the grave!" And with that he lit out through the brush, a-yelling "God save us!" at every jump. The boys ketched him and took him home in the wagon, but he was plumb out of his head. Doc says it was brain fever, and they finally pulled him through all right, but he ain't never been the same since.

That fellow still preaches around, but he ain't got the real power no more. There was a long time he never went near no funerals at all. You might see him projectin' round a buryin' sometimes, just the last few years, but he always stands away back from the grave hole. Yes sir, he sure does!

Stuck in a Holler Log

ONE TIME there was a Civil War veteran coming to town after his pension, when he seen a little speckled bobcat run into a holler log. A kitten bobcat is kind of cute, and the old man wanted to ketch the little feller alive, so he slid right in after it. But when he went to crawl back out his clothes got caught some way, so there he stuck tight in the

112

holler log. The old soldier wiggled and kicked till he was plumb wore out, but it didn't do no good. He says to himself this is a mighty miserable way for a man like me to die, but there ain't no help for it.

He just laid there and rested awhile, and he prayed a good deal. Whenever he heard a noise he would holler. Finally two old men come along, and they knowed who it was by his voice. Both of 'em had fought for the South, and they was bound to have their little joke. "Come on out, Yank," says one, "the shootin's all done now." And the other one says, "Don't be scared, Yank. We-uns ain't goin' to hurt you." The War had been over for more'n thirty years, but them old fellers was still talking about it. The old Federal says, "Pull me out of here, you goddam fools! This ain't no time for monkeyshines."

The Southerners didn't hurry themselves none, but finally they did try to pull him out. But he was stuck too tight, and they couldn't budge him. "Listen, neighbor," says one, "we'll have to split this here log open. You just take it easy, while we go get the choppin' axe." The old soldier was cussing pretty bad by this time. "Plug up the hole with rocks," says he. "If the old bobcat comes back after this young-un, she'll chaw my legs off!" So they piled up some rocks like he said.

While they was gone the old soldier squirmed around worse than ever, and all of a sudden he tore himself loose some way. So he kicked the rocks down and backed out. Then he piled the rocks up just like they was before. When the Johnnies got back they found him a-settin' there a-playin' with the little bobcat, which he had it wrapped up in what was left of his blue coat.

"For God's sake, how did you get out of the log?" they wanted to know.

"Well, boys," says he, "I just laid there a-thinkin' of all the bad things I ever done. I remembered them fellers I killed, an' the gals I lied to an' ruined, an' the money I stole from friends that trusted me. It didn't do no good, an' I was still stuck fast in that there log. But finally it come in my mind how I turned Democrat, an' voted for Cleveland in 1892. That done the job, gentlemen. It made me feel so small, I just crawled out through a knot hole!"

The Arkansas Traveler

ONE TIME there was a traveler way down in Arkansas, and he got lost in the big timber. It was a-coming on to rain, and the traveler was feeling mighty low. Pretty soon he come to a little cabin. There was an old-timer setting out in front, sawing away on a fiddle.

When the traveler rode up he says, "Hello," and the old-timer answered, "Hello yourself." Then he went right on a-fiddling, like this:

He just kept a-playing the same thing over and over.

"It looks like rain," says the traveler, "can I stay here all night?" The old-timer fiddled awhile, and then he says, "We ain't got no room. There ain't only one dry spot in the house, an' me an' Sal sleeps on that."

"Why don't you fix the roof?" the traveler says. "I cain't work in the rain," says the old-timer. "Well, why don't you fix it in dry weather?" The old man kept on a-fiddling. "In dry weather, it don't leak," says he.

"Have you got any spirits here?" asked the traveler. "We sure have," says the old-timer. "Sal seen one last night, an' it scared her pretty near to death." The traveler scowled. "I don't mean ghosts," says he, "I mean liquor." The old-timer fiddled awhile, then he says, "We had a mess of greens yesterday, an' I reckon there's some left in the pot." The traveler was getting kind of peevish. "I don't mean pot liquor, damn it! I mean drinkin' liquor. Have you got any whiskey?"

The old-timer fiddled awhile, and then he says, "Me an' Sal went shares an' bought a barrel last week. We sold it for ten cents a drink, cash on the barrelhead. We only had one dime between us, so every time Sal took a drink, she give me the dime. And whenever I took a drink, I give her the dime. Well, sir, the barrel's plumb empty now, an' Sal's got the dime. I have done quit sellin' whiskey, because there ain't no money in it."

The traveler thought about this awhile, and he seen the old-timer didn't have no head for business. So he says, "Why don't you play the rest of that tune?" The old-timer went right ahead with his fiddling. "This is a dance-tune, stranger. There ain't no rests in dance music." The traveler says, "I mean, why don't you play the balance of it?" The old-timer went right on a-fiddling. "It ain't got no balance," he says. "You don't understand," says the traveler. "Why don't you play the *fine part?*"

115

The old man stopped playing, and he says, "Stranger, can you play the fiddle?" The traveler says yes, and then he took the fiddle and played the same piece the old-timer was a-sawing away on. Then come the turn of the tune, and he played the fine part, like this:

The old-timer was so tickled, he jumped up and down like a colt. "Dick, take this gentleman's horse out to the barn; give him all the corn and fodder he can eat! Sal, fetch out the jug!" Soon as the traveler drunk some whiskey he begun to feel better. "Take half a dozen chairs, and make yourself at home," says the old-timer. "The old woman will cook us up a good supper directly. By God, stranger, you can stay here as long as you please! I'll give you plenty to eat and drink, and if it rains you can sleep in the dry spot!" The traveler drunk some more liquor and et a fine big supper, and then he fiddled pretty near all night. Finally he says, "My friend, can you tell me about the road I'm going to travel tomorrow?"

"Don't you worry about that," says the old-timer. "You just cross two or three big sloughs, and then ford the creek endways for a right smart piece. When you come to the place where the road forks, take either the right prong or the left. It don't make no difference, because both of 'em peters out pretty soon. About that time you better turn around, and you'll be lucky to find your way back to my house by supper time. So then we'll set right here, and you can fiddle just as long as you please!"

That's all there is to the story. But it stands to reason that the traveler got out to the big road some way and told the folks what happened at the old-timer's place. Because if he didn't, how would every jackleg fiddler in the country know all about it?

She Turned Him into a Pony

ONE TIME a fellow that lived up on Little Piney was just fallin' asleep when in come a pretty girl with a bridle in her hand. She give a whoop and jumped a-straddle of him, and quick as a wink he was turned into a pony. Away they went through the woods, and pretty soon they met up with some foreigners carrying sacks of gold money. It looked like they was bank robbers, or something.

The girl got down, and they put the gold onto the pony's back. After while they come to a cave and tied the pony to a tree, while they hid the money inside the cave somewhere. Then the girl rode back home, and next morning the fellow woke

117

up in his bed, but he was all tired and briar-scratched. The same thing happened three nights a-running, and the foreigners always carried gold into the same cave. And every morning the fellow was all tuckered out, with scratches on his legs and cockleburs in his hair. He didn't say nothing to the old woman about it, but he went to see a witch master at the forks of the creek. The witch master told him to mark the place where he was tied up. "Chaw a big blaze on the tree," says the witch master, "an' let fall as many droppin's as you can." Soon as the tree was marked so he could find it, the witch master was going to lay for the young witch and kill her with a silver bullet. Then they would get the gold money out of the cave, and split it fifty-fifty.

So the next night, when the young witch tied him up outside the cave, the fellow let fall as many droppin's as he could, and then he begun to chaw the tree so as to make a good blaze. All of a sudden he was back home in bed, and there come a big flash of light and a lot of hollering. It was the old woman that was a-hollering. And when the fellow woke up, what do you think? He'd done benastied the bed blankets, and pretty near bit the old woman's leg off!

Colonel Dockett

ONE TIME there was a man named Colonel Dockett. He wasn't really a colonel, just a blacksmith, but all the folks got to calling him Colonel anyhow. Colonel Dockett was a noted infidel, and he used to fight every preacher that come along.

118

We didn't have many church houses then, and mighty few regular ministers. But there was lots of Methodist and Baptist preachers that just rode around the country with Bibles and hymnbooks in their saddlebags. Folks called them circuit riders, and they would hold meetings wherever they got a chance. Colonel Dockett had whipped so many circuit riders that he was known all over the country, and preachers would go miles out of their way rather than pass his blacksmith shop.

One Saturday the blacksmith's helper says, "Here comes a preacher, Colonel!" Sure enough, there was a middle-aged man on a horse, and he was singing:

> We're marching to a glorious ground,
> We soon shall hear the trumpet sound,
> There'll be no sorrow, sin, or pain,
> And we'll never, never part again.

Colonel Dockett hurried out to the road and begun to sing "Twanky Diller" at the top of his voice. As soon as the preacher come along the Colonel grabbed his bridle. "Get down, preacher, an' take a lickin'," says he. "I whip every one of you fellows that dare to pass my place!"

The circuit rider looked him over for a minute. "All right, sinful brother," says he. "There ain't no sense in fightin'. But I can take punishment in a good cause, if it's forced on me." Then he jumped off his horse. Colonel Dockett swung clear from the ground, but the preacher dodged kind of awkward. And then he stepped in close and hit the Colonel twice, just two little short-arm jabs. Colonel Dockett was knocked plumb senseless, and just laid there in the road.

When the Colonel come to he was still laying there in the dust. The circuit rider was setting on a stump a-singing:

119

We're a-going home to bliss above,
Will you go? Will you go?
To dwell in mercy, peace, and love,
Will you go? Will you go?

The Colonel set up and felt his jaw, but he didn't have a word to say. Pretty soon the preacher climbed on his horse. "Farewell, sinful brother," says he. Then he rode off down the trail, and he was still a-singing.

Next night the preacher held a meeting at the crossroads, and Colonel Dockett was setting right down in front. And when sinners was invited to kneel at the altar, he was the first one on his knees. Pretty soon the Colonel stood up and sung "We're Going Home to Bliss Above" just as loud as anybody. He says if a good fighter like the parson believes in religion, there must be something to it.

After while somebody asked the preacher how he come to lick a big stout man like Colonel Dockett. The circuit rider tried to look meek, but he couldn't help grinning a little bit. "Brethren," says he, "in my sinful youth I used to be a prize fighter."

The Woman-Hater's Son

ONE TIME there was a man lived in a big town, and he was pretty well fixed. But his wife run off with some other fellow, and stole most of his money besides, so from then on he hated women. He took his little boy, that was about three years old, and built a shack away up in the mountains. A hired man packed in stuff so they could live comfortable, but the nearest neighbor was fifteen miles away, without no road. Him being a educated fellow, he learned the boy to read and write, but they never went nowhere. They never done nothing only hunt and fish, like a couple of wild Indians. When that boy was fourteen years old he didn't know what a woman looks like, and his father figured it was damn good riddance.

Finally the time come when the man had to go into town, to sign some papers or something. The boy wanted to go along, and his pappy give in, as there wasn't no easy way out of it. When they got to town the boy just walked around a-looking at things, because it was all new to him. Up to that day he thought all houses was just one-room cabins like him and his pappy lived in. He seen lots of things he didn't have no idea what they was, and his pappy told him about it as they went along.

Pretty soon the boy got to looking into the hardware store window, and the old man was explaining what all that truck was good for. Just then here come a pretty girl a-walking down the street. She showed her legs and wiggled her bottom surprising, like them town girls do. "What's that, Pappy?" says the boy. "That's a devil red-hot from Hell," growls the old man, and then he went on talking about them things in the hardware store. The boy didn't say no more, but he just stood there a-looking at the pretty girl till she was plumb out of sight.

They fooled around the wagon yard awhile and went into the courthouse and the hotel and the harness shop and the livery stable. The old man bought new shirts and overalls for both of them, and shoes too, and some candy. They drunk a couple bottles of beer, which was something the boy never had tasted before, but he didn't like it much. Then the old man

121

says, "Son, I want to buy you a nice present. How about a new pump shotgun, with shells enough to last all winter?" But the boy says he don't care for no pump gun, because the old single-barrel suits him all right. Well, the old man says does he want a pony, with a fine saddle and bridle like they seen in the harness shop? But the boy don't seem to take no interest in ponies.

Finally the old man says, "Listen, son, we've got plenty of money in the bank. You can have just about anything you like." The boy looked up and down the street. "Pappy," says he, "there ain't but one thing in this town that I want." The

122

old man says for him to speak up, because it's about time they was starting for home. "Well, Pappy," the boy says, "get me one of them devils red-hot from Hell!"

It just goes to show that boys is all alike, no matter where they live at. You can't get away from nature just by hiding out in the woods somewhere.

Gunpowder Seed

ONE TIME there was a bunch of Indians that didn't know much about white people. They hunted with bows and blowguns mostly, but some of the young bucks had got old smoothbore muskets. The Indians knowed how to make slugs, and they would use pebbles if there wasn't no lead handy, but they didn't have no idea what gunpowder was made out of. The only way for them to get powder was to swap with the white traders that come along every once in a while.

Finally a buffalo hunter told the Indians that gunpowder come from big farms back east, where the Yankees raise it just like squashes. He showed 'em a seed he carried in his pocket. It was a black ball, about half an inch through. The Indians licked the ball with their tongue, and they seen it was nothing but a piece of candy that folks used to call jawbreakers. The buffalo hunter says the candy is just put on for fertilizer to make it grow, and the powder seed is inside. The old chief grunted contemptuous, and throwed it in the fire. In about a minute the thing went off BANG, and scattered hot ashes all over the place. So them Indians wanted to trade for gunpowder seeds

123

right now, and pretty soon the buffalo hunter had two pony-loads of beaver, with some prime otter skins throwed in for greens. The Indians didn't get nothing but a little poke of jaw-breaker candy. It was just plain candy, because the sample they throwed in the fire was the only one that had any powder in it.

The Indians planted them seeds mighty careful, with a dead fish in every hill to richen up the dirt. The squaws pulled weeds and carried water all summer, but nothing didn't come up. The old chief seen how they had been played for a sucker, but he never made no complaint.

When the next bunch of traders come along, the Indians took all their stuff, and never give the traders nothing. When the traders begun to holler how they was robbed the old chief says it ain't so, because his white brothers will get lots of fur pretty soon. The traders says well, how long have we got to wait? "Just a little while," says the old chief. "My people will pay for everything, just as soon as the gunpowder is ripe."

Them traders was a long time getting back to the settlement, because they had to walk all the way. The old-timers said they was lucky to get home without losing their hair. And maybe they was, at that.

Willie Up the Chimney

ONE TIME there was a fellow heard about how his wife was running around with Willie Weaver, and he didn't like it. So he come home through the woods un-expected, and there was Willie's horse tied out behind the

124

pawpaw patch, so he thought Willie must be in the house. The door was locked, and his wife says, "Who is it?" The fellow told her who it was mighty quick, so she opened the door. But when he went in, Willie Weaver wasn't nowhere in sight. His wife says, "What are you doing with that knife? And what are you looking under the bed for?" But he didn't return no answer.

The fellow thought about it awhile, and he figured out where Willie was a-hiding. So then he cut the bedtick open and pulled out a lot of straw. His wife says, "You must have went crazy." But he just throwed the straw in the fireplace and touched a match to it. Pretty soon you could hear a hell of a racket in the chimney, and down come Willie Weaver. He was black as tar, like one of these here chimney swallows. His eyes was full of soot, so he couldn't see nothing. Willie figured he was going to get cut sure, and the woman was a-hollering like a steam whistle.

The fellow just looked at her and Willie Weaver a minute, and he shut his knife and put it in his pocket. Then he took a stick of wood and beat poor Willie within a inch of his life. Probably he would have beat him plumb to death, only some folks come along the road and heard all that hollering and screeching. They drug Willie out and put him on his horse, but he was hurt too bad to ride, so they had to haul him home in a wagon.

After the folks was gone the fellow's wife says she is going to cut his throat the first time she catches him asleep. But he says if you do they will hang you sure, because all them people will testify what happened here tonight. And then she says, "If I was to take your scalp to the courthouse they will pay me a bounty, just like it was a wildcat!" So one word led to another, and pretty soon he give her a good beating too. Them

125

people never got along very good, because it seemed like him and her was always a-quarreling about something. But they didn't have no more trouble about Willie Weaver, anyhow.

His Voice Was A-Changing

ONE TIME there was a boy driving a skittish team, and when a piece of paper blowed across the road it scared 'em, so they run away with him. The next thing he knowed they turned the wagon over and broke loose. The boy wasn't hurt, but there he was a-laying in the road, with the wagon on top of him. He pushed his best, but he wasn't stout enough to lift the wagon so's to get out from under.

Whenever he heard anybody a-coming, the boy would holler for help. But the folks never thought about anybody being under a wagon that was upside down. Most of them was pretty drunk anyhow on account of the Crane Picnic, and they never paid no attention.

Finally a old man come along afoot, and he could hear the hollering plain enough. But the boy's voice was a-changing, and it was what they call in the goslin's. So first he would holler "Help!" in a fine tenor. And the next minute he would holler "Help!" again, only this time it sounded like a big coarse bass voice.

The old man listened at it awhile, and then he says, "If two men ain't got gumption enough to turn over a wagon-bed, let the damn fools stay where they are at!"

And so then he just tromped on down the road and left the boy a-hollering under the wagon.

126

Too Much Powder

ONE TIME there was a fellow run a little store. There wasn't no bank in town, so the folks would give him their money to keep in his big iron safe. Pretty soon some robbers come and prized the safe open and stole the people's money. There wasn't no insurance in them days, so the fellow had to pay it out of his own pocket. Then he bought a new safe, but in about six months the robbers come back again and knocked the knob off with a sledge hammer. They didn't get much money this time, because our night marshal heard the noise and he run them out of town.

The fellow that kept the store was pretty goddam mad, and he says you just wait, as I am going to fix these son-of-a-bitches, and the next time they will get the surprise of their life. Then he bought another safe, and set it right up in front where every-body could see how heavy it was.

Things went along for about a year, and then just before daylight come a explosion that busted window glass all over town. It blowed the whole front out of the store building. There was two dead men a-laying in the street, and one of them was a woman dressed up in men's clothes. Plenty of folks knowed who they was, all right, but nobody said anything. The safe was tore wide open, but it was plumb empty. The marshal couldn't make out what the hell happened, and neither could anybody else.

When the sheriff come from the county seat he says them

dead people was robbers all right, because they had soaped a crack in the safe and poured in nitroglycerine to blow the door off. You could see where they had fastened the cap on with this here adhesive tape. "It looks like they put in too much powder," says the sheriff, "but I don't see how come there ain't no money scattered around." The fellow that run the store says it is because he never keeps no money in the safe. "I have lost confidence in safes, after being robbed twice," says he. "Every night I put the money and papers in the old iron powder-box out back of the store. There's a good stout padlock on it."

The folks just kind of studied about this awhile, and then the sheriff says, "Where do you keep your dynamite, then? It's ag'in the law to leave explosives a-layin' around loose." The fellow that run the store grinned. "I don't leave no explosives around loose," says he. "I always put the dynamite in the safe, of a night."

The sheriff and the marshal just stood there a-looking at him. But they didn't ask no more questions. Pretty soon some of the dead woman's kinfolks come and got the bodies and buried them in the Chicken Ridge graveyard. And that's all there is to the story.

A Long-Handled Shovel

ONE TIME there was a fool boy up on Cow Creek took a notion to dig him a well in the pasture. He dug down a ways, and then all of a sudden the side of the well caved in. There was some rocks fell down too, and it's God's own luck the poor halfwit didn't get killed and buried right there.

Away along in the night he come a-running up to one of the neighbors' house, a-hollering so loud he woke everybody up. "For God's sake," says he, "give me a long-handled shovel!" The old man says this is a hell of a time to raise such a hulla-baloo, and if you want to borrow something why don't you come in the daytime? But the boy just kept on a-hollering. "The well caved in on me! I'm a-dyin' under all them rocks an' dirt! For God's sake give me a long-handled shovel!" The old man was pretty mad by this time. "I ain't goin' to put up with no more of this foolishness," he says. "Maw, fetch me the shotgun!" And so the boy run a-blubbering down the road.

When he come to the next house the boy hollered every-body up just like he done before. "For God's sake," says he, "give me a long-handled shovel! The well caved in on me! I'm a-dyin' under all them rocks an' dirt! For God's sake give me a long-handled shovel!" The man come to the door and opened it, until he seen who was there. "You ain't a-dyin'," says he, "you're just drunk." And then the man went back to bed and blowed out the light. The boy hollered around outside for awhile. Then he give up and run on down the road.

It was pretty near daylight when he come to the third house, and the fellow that lived there got up and put on his clothes. "For God's sake give me a long-handled shovel!" says the boy. "The well caved in on me! I'm a-dyin' under all them rocks an' dirt! For God's sake give me a long-handled shovel!" The fellow couldn't make no sense out of what the boy says, but he figured something serious was the matter. So he went and got the shovel. The boy grabbed it and run back up the road fast as he could.

129

The fellow that give him the shovel follered right along behind, to help out. They run pretty near four miles. Then the boy took out across the cow pasture and jumped down a big hole in the ground. Dirt and rocks begun to fly, so the fellow just stood back out of the way. He figured on doing some shoveling himself, soon as the boy got tired. Pretty soon the boy come a-climbing out. He wiped the dirt and sweat off his face, and he looked mighty happy about something. "By God, I made it!" says he. "But it was a mighty close call. If you hadn't give me that shovel, I'd be dead as a wagon-tire right this minute!"

The fellow stared at the boy mighty funny for awhile, and then he went over and looked down the hole. "Listen, son," says he, "was anybody else down there, when the dirt caved in?" The boy says, "No, I was all by myself. That's what makes well-digging so goddam dangerous."

Nobody said anything after that, and you could hear the peter-birds a-singing in the trees. The fellow just set there and thought about it awhile. Pretty soon he picked up his shovel and started out to walk the four miles back home.

The Green Man in the Tree

ONE TIME there was a fellow that was raised up on Bee Creek, but he had went to the Territory for two or three years. After he come back he always wore a big white hat, so everybody would know he'd been out West, and he kept a-talking about Oklahoma all the time. The folks didn't

130

like to see a young man act that way, but he come of a good family and they figured maybe he would outgrow it.

It was on the way to a dance the fellow run into something bad, and here he come home at a dead run. He jumped off and left the horse a-standing in the road, with the saddle and bridle still on it. He got in bed and put his head under the covers. Didn't even stop to undress, and you could see them cowboy boots with big spurs sticking right through the blankets. His six-shooter was on the floor with three chambers empty, and his hat was plumb gone. The folks took care of his pony and ask him what was the matter, but he wouldn't talk to nobody. Just laid there and shivered pretty near all night.

Next morning they give him some black coffee with whiskey in it. And after while he says, "Boys, come with me, because I might need help." So they all went down by the schoolhouse. There was an old black-oak tree, with one big limb a-sticking out over the road. The fellow says that when he rode under that tree last night, in the bright moonshine, he heard a little chirp. And when he looked up, there was a man setting a-straddle of that big limb. "Boys, it wasn't no natural man," the fellow says. "He was green as a tree-frog, from head to foot. Even his goddam hair was green! His clothes fit him tight as a glove, or else he didn't have no clothes on." The boys all looked kind of funny, but they didn't say nothing.

"I spoke to him civil," the fellow went on, "but that there green man just chirped like a chipmunk. Then I told him to come down, but he just laughed at me. So I out with my gun and shot him three times." The boys could see where one of them big forty-five bullets had tore a chunk out of the limb.

"Well sir," the fellow says, "he wasn't six foot off. If he was a natural man I'd have gutted him sure, but that green son-of-a-bitch just grinned. All of a sudden the varmint swung down and grabbed my hat and slapped it right in my pony's face. The pony run like a deer and never stopped till we got plumb home." The boys looked around, and sure enough they found the fellow's big white hat in a ditch. There was some green marks on the brim of it, like fingerprints, but probably they was just grass stains.

The folks took the big hat home, but the fellow never did wear it no more. He gave up talking about Oklahoma, too. That green thing wasn't no natural man, and he taken it as a warning. The fellow kind of settled down after that, and he's one of the best citizens we ever had in this county. But nobody ever seen him ride up that schoolhouse road again, even in broad daylight.

Cornbread and Bacon

ONE TIME there was some people that was very poor, and they didn't have nothing to eat only cornbread. One day the old man come home, and he had got hold of a little piece of bacon. But it wouldn't do for them to gobble it all up at once, he says. So they just hung the bacon up on a string over the table. When they set down to eat, everybody could reach up and rub his dodger on the bacon. And they all says how fine it is to have meat with their bread, just like rich people.

The kids went to school and there wasn't nothing in their

132

buckets only hard cornbread without no shortening, but they told the other children how they had meat for supper every night. There was a good deal of talk about it in the neighborhood, and everybody thought them folks set a mighty good table. Some people says they was living too extravagant and would likely end up in the poorhouse.

One of the boys come home early from school, and he was pretty hungry. He found a little piece of cold cornbread, and started to rub it on the bacon. But the old woman seen him. "You quit that, Johnny," she says. "It ain't healthy for children to fill up on bread an' meat between meals. Do you want to founder yourself?" So then she snatched him away from the table and paddled him good.

Second Sight

ONE TIME there was a man and his name was Coonrod, but the boys called him Coon for short. He claimed he used to be a preacher, and he was a pretty fair jackleg lawyer, too. Sometimes he says he is a doctor, that could cure pretty near anybody no matter what ailed 'em. He knowed how to conjure hornets, and spook fish, and tell fortunes, and witch water, and find buried treasure. He had second sight, too. If anybody had something in a box, or all wrapped up in paper, he could just look at it and tell you what was inside. It was bragging about this here second sight that got Coonrod into a awful tight place up on Bull Creek.

The folks up that way was tough as a boot, and they was all

natural born gamblers. You could see fellows a-playin' euchre and pitch and old sledge and poker all along the road, with crapshooters in every fence corner. Them people had foot races and rooster fights and fox chases and shootin' matches and horseshoe pitchin's and prize fights and dancin' contests and gander pullin's and debates and marble games. They bet big money on everything that come along. One of them Bull Creek possum hunters lost two hundred dollars right in the schoolhouse, a-betting on a goddam spellin' bee.

Big Ike Lewis come a-riding in one day, and he says, "Coonrod, they tell me you can look at a box and tell what's inside of it." Coonrod says, "Ike, it's the God's truth," and then he begun to brag how he is the seventh son of a seventh son, born in the dark of the moon with a veil on his face besides. He says he can look at Brewer's cash drawer and tell how much money is in it, right down to the last penny. He says if you show him a closed coffin he can tell whether the corpse is a man or a woman, and how old they are, and what they died of. And then he begun to tell about some other things he could do, but Big Ike cut him short. "Get on your horse," says he, and up the Bull Creek road they went.

When they come to the old Jeffers place there was a big crowd of people out back of the house. They had a old black kettle turned upside down on the ground, with a heavy rock on top of it. Old man Jeffers was a-settin' right beside the kettle, and everybody else a-standing well back. "Listen, Coonrod," says Big Ike, "nobody knows what's in that kettle only Mister Jeffers. I've bet my team and wagon against five hundred dollars that you can tell what it is."

Coonrod begun to sweat like a bound boy at a shuckin' match. He didn't have no more idea what was under that kettle than the man in the moon. "If you tell what it is," says Big Ike, "I'm going to give you fifty dollars for your trouble. But if you make me lose my team and wagon, I'm going to cut your guts out right here! And then I'm a-going to fill your paunch up with rocks, and throw the corpse in the river!" says he.

The fellows that was standing around looked plumb wolfish, and Coonrod was scared goddam near to death. He knowed what kind of a man Big Ike Lewis was, and he wouldn't put nothing past that Bull Creek crowd. He walked round the kettle two or three times, but how could anybody figure out what was in it? There wasn't no use lyin' now, so Coonrod couldn't do nothing but give up and hope for the best.

"Well, Mister Jeffers," says he, "it looks like you got old Coon this time."

Big Ike stepped forward like he was going to butcher poor Coonrod right now, but old man Jeffers just set there with his mouth open. "It cain't be!" says old man Jeffers. "It ain't possible!" says he, and his face turned plumb green. Big Ike looked from one to the other. "Mister Jeffers," he says very polite, "will you please to turn over that there kettle?" The old man never moved, but two of them Bull Creek boys lifted the rock and turned the kettle on one side. And there set a big old boar coon, with both front feet in a steel trap!

Old man Jeffers looked like he was a-dying, but finally he out with his wallet and paid Ike Lewis five hundred dollars. Big Ike handed over fifty dollars to Coonrod, and that's all there was to it.

But the folks say Coonrod kind of quietened down after that. He never done no more braggin' around them Bull Creek boys, anyhow.

The Fancy Pot

ONE TIME there was a fellow that lived away back in the hills, and he went to see a rich man in town. The rich man had a big house with fine furniture, and thick carpets, and servants all over the place. They set down to talk awhile, but the country fellow was chewing tobacco, and pretty soon he had to spit. There wasn't no fireplace in the room, so he just spit in a corner and went right on a-talking.

The rich man didn't say anything, but he nodded to a servant. The servant went out and got a hand-painted spittoon, and he set it down right where the country boy spit. The country fellow didn't pay no attention at the time, but when he wanted to spit again he seen the fancy spittoon setting there. So this time he spit over in another corner of the room. The servant picked up the spittoon and moved it over to the second corner. The boy from the country scowled at this, but he went on a-talking just the same.

Pretty soon the mountain man had to spit again, and this time he let her go right on the carpet. So the servant carried the cuspidor over there and set it down in front of him.

The country boy was mad now, and he scowled worse than ever. "I don't know what you're a-doing with that fancy pot," says he. "But if you move it one more time, I'm a-going to spit right *in* the goddam thing!"

Alf Bolen's Head

ONE TIME there was a young fellow named Alf Bolen, from somewhere down in southeast Missouri. When the War come along Alf talked loud for the South, but he never joined the Confederate army. He just got together a gang of ruffians and they went around killing people, and burning houses, and stealing anything they could get their hands on. They would burn old women's feet to make 'em tell where their money was hid, and cut children's ears off, and all such as that.

The Federal troops done everything they could to catch

Bolen, and so did the Home Guard, but they never had no luck. The soldiers did capture one of Bolen's gang, though. They took him up to Springfield and was fixing to hang him. But the fellow's wife rode all the way from Taney county, and she told the officers that if they would turn her husband loose she'd help 'em get Alf Bolen. One of the Federal soldiers put on a Confederate uniform and went with the woman. They found Alf in a farmhouse just south of the Arkansas line. None of his gang was with him, just a young girl and two old women. When Bolen set down to eat dinner the Federal shot him from behind. They didn't take no chances with fellows like Alf Bolen in them days.

The soldier didn't know Bolen by sight, so he couldn't tell if he'd got the right man or not. The woman that brought him down there said it was Alf Bolen, but all the neighbors declared it wasn't. So the woman cut the dead man's head off and put it in a sack. Then her and the soldier started back to Springfield. When they got into Christian county they met up with some of the Iowa First that had seen Bolen lots of times. The woman showed 'em the head, and they says yes, that's him all right.

So then the soldiers stuck Alf Bolen's head on the end of a pole and marched around town like it was a flag. Next they went up to Springfield and paraded up and down the streets. Bolen had lots of friends in Springfield, and some of them felt pretty bad when they seen his head stuck up on a pole that way. But the soldiers just laughed, and they says it won't be long now till we'll have Jeff Davis's head on a pole too.

Some of the folks buried Alf down near Forsyth, but they didn't have no preacher, and it seemed kind of heathenish to bury a man without no head. The soldiers carried the head around till it got to smelling funky, and then they just throwed it to the hogs. Them soldiers was a awful tough lot. They come from Iowa mostly, and Illinois.

Most everybody has forgot all them things nowadays, of course. But twenty years after the War, right here in Stone county, children used to take a pumpkin and cut holes in it, to look like eyes and nose and mouth. And then they would put in straw for whiskers and stick the pumpkin on the end of a pole. And if anybody was to ask what they was a-doing, they'd say, "We're a-playin' Alf Bolen!"

The Girl and the Road Agent

ONE TIME there was a man that didn't do no work, as he just loaned out money at big interest. He didn't trust nobody but his own daughter, and she was a big stout girl about sixteen year old. Some folks over east of town had paid off their mortgage, and the girl was a-carrying the money home to her pappy. It was small bills and silver, in a little paper sack.

She was walking along tending to her own business, when here come a road agent all dressed up. He says, "Howdy," and then all of a sudden he jumped off'n his horse and grabbed her from behind. Most of her dress was tore off right now, but she kicked the fellow in the belly and yelled like a steam engine. When she seen he was getting the best of her, the girl tore the poke and scattered silver dollars all over the place. The road agent dropped her like a hot potater and begun to pick up the money. The girl just laid still for a minute, and then she jumped on his big horse and away she went. The road agent run and hollered and fired his pistol, but he didn't hit nothing.

When the girl got home the old man says what on earth do you mean, riding around the country half-naked? And whose horse is that, and where is the money for the mortgage? She told him what happened, and they looked in the saddlebags. And what do you think? Them saddlebags was plumb full of gold and silver! Finally her pappy says, "Are you hurt?" and she told him no. So then the old man says, "Daughter, you have done a fine day's work, because there is ten times as much money in the saddlebags as you had in the paper poke. And we got a good horse besides, with a fine saddle and bridle to boot."

And that's the way it was, too. Because if a fellow is a road

140

agent he can't go hollering to the law, or else the sheriff might want to know where he got all that gold and silver. And maybe there is a reward out for him besides. Also the girl would tell the jury how this man attackted her and tore her clothes off, so he'd be throwed in the jailhouse for seventy years' hard labor. It just goes to show that honesty pays off in the long run, like the old man says.

Played for a Sucker

ONE TIME a gang of boys went a-gigging on White River, down by the riffle they call Nelly's Apron. There was five of 'em, all named Turner. Two of them was brothers, and the others was cousins. That whole country is full of Turners, but these fellows was old fishin' pardners. They had been giggin' together ever since they was big enough to push a johnboat.

Some of 'em was better giggers than others, of course. But that didn't make no difference, because they always divided up the catch anyhow. After they got the fish all cleaned, they put 'em in five piles on the gravel-bar. Then Sol would turn his back, and Poggy would point to a pile and holler, "Whose is this'n?" and Sol would sing out "Jim's" or "Bill's" or whatever name come into his head. The old-timers always divided up their fish that way, so everybody got a fair share.

This particular night, the fish was runnin' small. There was a nice catfish and one big redhorse, but the rest of 'em didn't amount to much. Mostly hogmolly suckers, and little 'uns at

141

that. When they went to divide up, Sol got the cat and Poggy drawed the redhorse. Nate Turner looked mighty sour. He'd killed both of them big 'uns, but all he got was a mess of hog-mollies. Nate never said nothing, but he done a lot of thinking. And next day he told Jim and Bill what he was a-thinking about.

It was more'n a week after that when the Turners went gigging again. Nate seen that two piles of fish was noticeable better'n the others. And then him and Jim and Bill watched everything mighty close. When Sol come to one of the little messes he hollered, "Whose is this'n?" and Poggy sung out, "Bill's." And then Sol pointed at one of the big piles, and he hollered, "Well, whose is this'n?" and Poggy says, "Mine." Nate looked at Jim and Bill, but Sol never noticed anything wrong. He just went over to another little mess of fish. "Whose is this'n?" says he. And Poggy sung out, "Jim's." Next Sol come to the biggest heap of all, and he says, "Well, whose is this'n?" And Poggy, with his back turned all the time, speaks right up. "Yourn," says he.

Jim and Bill Turner wasn't very smart, but they seen the bug under the chip, all right. It was Sol saying "Well" that done it. You'd think such a trick wouldn't fool nobody, but Nate and Jim and Bill was played for a sucker year after year. That's how come them boys was so goddam mad, to think how easy they'd been took in. Bill Turner would have killed somebody sure, if Nate hadn't kicked the knife out of his hand. They beat Sol and Poggy damn near to death and left 'em a-laying on the gravel-bar.

The whole bunch carried guns for a long time after that, and Nate used to show his teeth like a wolf whenever he seen Sol and Poggy. Some of the neighbors figured there was going to be a feud that would split the Turner clan wide open. They was all kinfolks though, and blood's thicker'n water, so finally they just let it pass. But there was bad feeling amongst 'em as long as them boys lived. And right down to this day, the Turners don't do no giggin' together on White River.

The Cowpokes Told a Tale

ONE TIME there was two fellows from the Territory come to town. They was dressed like cowpokes, and the biggest one claimed to be a broncho twister. Anyhow, they talked a lot of horse, and not like these here rodeo cowboys neither. Both of 'em had money, and they was stepping high, wide, and handsome. They hung around the honkytonks for about a week, and then one morning they showed up missing.

Two or three days after that they come to town again, and you wouldn't hardly have knowed 'em. They was bit, scratched, bruised, and skun from head to foot; their hats was gone, and their clothes a-hanging in tatters. The girls washed the blood off and got 'em some new shirts and levis. Them boys had spent their money free at the Pea Green House, so the girls didn't ask no questions. But after he got a few drinks the bronc rider told the folks what happened.

The fellow says him and his pardner went out in the hills to look for some money that was buried under a rock, and they met the Devil right in the road. He was seven foot tall and black, with split hoofs and a forked tail just like in the picture books. The Devil told 'em he was fixing to eat their meat and throw their bones to the buzzards, and then he would carry their souls to Hell. It was a terrible fight, but finally them cowpokes throwed the Old Boy down and hog-tied him with his own galluses. They took their knife and altered him like a boar hog, and notched his ears, and bobbed off his tail besides. The big fellow dehorned him, and soon as the runnin'-iron was hot the little one drawed a Tee-Bar-See on his flank. All this time the old Devil was a-blowing smoke and bellering so you could hear him ten mile off. Soon as they got him branded the cowpokes started a-driving the varmint to town, so they could saddle him and show off before the Pea Green girls. But the Old Boy broke loose at the crossroads and went a-whooping off through the woods towards Little Hominy.

Well, sir, we got plenty of big liars right here in town, but none of 'em ever told such a tale as that. The fellow that claimed he was a bronc peeler seen everybody looked pretty doubtful. "I've always heard tell how the Devil's breath is pure sulphur," says he, "and damn if I don't believe there's something to it." With that he pulled a handful of money out of his pocket, and every one of them silver dollars was turned plumb black!

The boys and girls just set still for a long time, with their mouth wide open. They didn't know what to think. After while some fellows went out to look for sign at the crossroads, but they couldn't see nothing. Nobody ever did find out where them two cowpokes had been, or how they got skinned up, or what it was turned their money black like that.

The Three Dreams

ONE TIME there was three boys went a-hunting, and they was getting awful hungry. They hunted and they hunted, but the ground was too dry, and the dogs didn't work good, and the moon wasn't right for hunting anyhow. So they only got one possum, and it was a mighty small possum at that.

Finally the boys was so tired and hungry they couldn't hunt no more. They built a fire and put the possum on to cook. Pretty soon the biggest boy says, "If we split that possum three ways, there won't ary one of us get enough." The second boy says, "That's right, but what can we do about it?" The biggest boy says, "Let's all lay down and sleep while the possum is a-cooking, and whichever has the best dream can eat the whole possum." The middle-sized boy says, "Well, I reckon it's better for two of us to starve than three." And the least boy says, "If that's what you fellows want to do, it's all right with me." So they laid down beside the fire to sleep.

When they woke up it was broad daylight, and the biggest boy says, "I drempt the Government raffled off Arkansas, an' I won the whole damn state!" The second boys says, "I drempt that God died of smallpox, an' Judge Thornton read the will, an' He left all Creation to me!" The least boy says, "Well, I reckon you win. My dream didn't amount to nothin', alongside them that you fellers had." So then they drug out the possum, but there wasn't a bit of meat left on the carcass, and the bones was sucked plumb white.

The middle-sized boy was pretty mad, because he'd won that possum fair and square. Pretty soon he noticed the least boy's chin looked uncommon greasy. "I ain't accusing nobody," says he, "but what did *you* dream about?" The third boy says, "Oh, my dream ain't hardly worth telling. I just drempt I got up and et that little possum. Maybe I kind of walked in my sleep," he says.

The other boys just set there and cussed him for everything they could lay their tongue to. They was mighty mad, but there wasn't nothing to be done about it. So after while they got up and took out for home, to get a bait of victuals. And that's all there is to the story.

Corn for the Miller

ONE TIME there was a farm boy a-riding to mill with a grinding of corn in a big old tow-sack. He had the corn in one end of the sack and a rock in the other, so it balanced nice across the saddle.

A smart-aleck from town come along, and he says your pony is about done for, and it ain't sensible to put rocks on his back. The farm boy just grinned. "My pappy always done it this way," says he, "and so did grandpappy before him. What's good enough for them is good enough for me." And then the farm boy rode on, but he kept a-thinking about what the fellow said.

Pretty soon here come another smart-aleck, and he says you have got that poor animal loaded too heavy. No horse ought to carry a boy and a big rock and a sack of corn besides, says he. "Maybe you're right," says the farm boy. "But I got to take this here corn to mill, and I need the rock to balance it. The only thing that can be took off the horse is me." So then he got down and walked, a-leading the pony, with the corn hanging down on one side of the saddle and the rock hanging down on the other side.

Pretty soon here come the third smart-aleck, and he says the pony can't hardly stand up, because all that rock and corn is too much for him. And it's a shame for a big stout boy to be walking along like you ain't got a care in the world! "Maybe you're right," says the farm boy. "I will tote the stuff myself awhile, an' let the horse have a rest." So he pulled the sack off'n the saddle and put it on his back.

It was a hot day, and pretty soon the farm boy begun to get tired. "I don't mind packing the weight," says he to himself, "it's this here walkin' that's destroyin' me." So then he got into the saddle again, but he was still carrying the corn and the rock on his shoulders.

When the miller seen them a-coming he begun to laugh. "What for are you carryin' the corn on your back?" says he. "It's too heavy for the poor horse, so I'm a-helping him out," says the farm boy. The miller laughed louder than ever when he heard that, but he didn't say nothing more. The farm boy set down on a pile of cobs while the corn was a-grinding, and he thought about it a long time. Finally he figured out what the miller was a-laughing at. "I believe them three smart-alecks has made a fool out of me," says he to himself.

Next time he went to mill the farm boy carried his corn

147

across the saddle with a rock in the other end of the sack, just like his pappy and his grandpappy done before him. Pretty soon one of them smart-alecks come along, and he says carrying extra weight is wasteful; it would be more economical to take the rock out and put half the corn in each end of the sack.

"Yes, I reckon it would be a saving," says the farm boy. "But when this rock wears out all I got to do is pick up another one. There's plenty of 'em in our pasture, and we don't give a damn for expenses." So then he rode on and left the smart-aleck a-standing there with his mouth open.

The Drummer's Magic Circle

ONE TIME there was some people run a hotel. It wasn't a very good one, but it was the only hotel in town, so all the salesmen had to stay there over night.

There was one drummer from Springfield that was a kind of sissy fellow, and he always looked like he just come out of a bandbox. When the girl went to clean up his room next morning, she found something mighty funny. The bed hadn't been slept in, and there was a big circle on the bare floor, made out of stuff which it looked like molasses. She called the fellow that owned the hotel to come and look, but he didn't know what to make of it, neither. He'd been running the hotel for a long time, but he never seen nothing like that before. They had quite a time scrubbing the molasses off the floor.

In about two weeks the sissy drummer come back, and the same thing happened again. Nobody said a word, but the folks studied about it a lot, and some thought he must be fooling with witch's business. The girls in the hotel kind of hinted around, but the sissy drummer wouldn't have nothing to do with them. So that's the way it went all summer, till finally one morning he went to check out. "I won't be making this town any more," he says to the man that owned the hotel, "because they have give me a new territory down around Little Rock." The hotel man says would you mind telling me something? "Not at all," answered the sissy drummer, "and what is it you want to know?" So then the man that owned the hotel says, "I would like to know why you always make that big circle on the floor of your room."

The sissy drummer laughed pretty loud, and picked up his suitcase. "Well," says he, "I'm a man that can't abide bedbugs. So I carry my own blanket in my grip, and a whisk broom, and a box of bug powder, and a quart of molasses. I just sweep a clean place on the floor and scatter bug powder on it. Then I make a big circle with the molasses, spread down my clean blanket, and that's where I sleep. There ain't money enough in this country to hire me to lay on one of your beds." And with that the sissy drummer walked out.

The hotel man never told a living soul, but one of the girls was listening to what the fellow said, and it was all over town in no time. The boys down at the drugstore laughed theirself sick, and the people that run the hotel never did hear the last of it.

Good Dogs Cost Money

ONE TIME there was a fellow from Kansas City come a-driving along in his big car, as he was going fishing down in Arkansas somewhere. When he got into the rough country south of Branson he come around a curve pretty fast, and all of a sudden he run over a red bird-dog. The fellow stopped and got out of his car, but the setter was plumb dead. There wasn't a house in sight, but he seen a mountain man a-standing by the road, with a big Winchester in his hand.

Men that hunt with bird-dogs don't carry rifles, and the city fellow was kind of uneasy. "Well sir, I'm afraid I run over your dog," he says. "I'm mighty sorry it happened. Being a bird hunter myself, I know that good dogs cost money nowadays." The mountain man just nodded, and shifted the Winchester to the slack of his arm. The fellow from Kansas City pulled out a wallet and counted off five ten-dollar bills. "Take this fifty dollars," says he, "it will help you to get another dog." The mountain man didn't say nothing, but he took the money and put it in his pocket.

The Kansas City fellow begun to breathe a little easier. "Well, I must be going, because I've got a long drive ahead of me," he says. "I'm sorry I spoiled your day's hunting." The mountain man grinned a little. "That's all right, Mister," says he. "I didn't figure on huntin' today, nohow. I was just goin' down the Holler a piece, to shoot that egg-suckin' dog."

Three Barrels of Whiskey

ONE TIME there was three brothers named Matthew, Mark, and Luke. They helped a moonshiner out of a awful bad mess. If it wasn't for what them three brothers done, that moonshiner would have went to the penitentiary, sure. After everything blowed over and settled down, the moonshiner come a-driving into town, and he give Matthew a barrel of good whiskey.

It looks like a barrel of whiskey would last all winter. But Mark and Luke come over to sample the stuff, and pretty soon some of their kinfolks dropped in. All three of them boys was married, so here come a lot of their wife's kinfolks, too. They fetched fried chicken and ham and cake and all kind of victuals. There was a fiddler happened to come along that night, and so they give a big dance. It wasn't no time at all till Matthew's whiskey was plumb gone.

Two or three weeks afterwards the moonshiner come a-driving into town again, and this time he give Mark a barrel of good whiskey. Luke and Matthew come over to sample the stuff, of course, and some of their wife's kinfolks got wind of it. Pretty soon they was having a big jamboree, dancing and drinking and hell-raising just like they done before. It wasn't no time at all till Mark's whiskey was plumb gone.

Two or three weeks after that the moonshiner come a-driving in with a barrel of good whiskey for Luke. This time all three brothers got together, and they figured out a way to keep that whiskey in the family. "Listen, Luke," says Matthew, "soon as it gets dark you hide the barrel somewheres. Then tomorrow you can tell them greedy-guts that somebody must have stole it." Mark nodded his head. "All you got to do," he says, "is to tell a straight story and put on a good act." Luke studied about it awhile, and then he says all right.

Soon as it got dark Luke rolled the barrel out in his pasture and piled some brush over it. Matthew and Mark was hid in the woods a-watching him. After Luke went back to the house they siphoned off the whiskey in jugs and buried the jugs in a cave down by the river. Them boys figured it was the best thing to do. They knowed poor Luke couldn't hold out ag'in his wife and her kinfolks.

Next day folks come from all over the country, and they was a-milling around Luke's house like bees round a sorghum mill. He told 'em somebody had stole the whiskey, but they didn't believe it, so finally he give up and went out to the brush pile. When he seen the barrel was empty Luke begun to holler louder'n anybody. "We been robbed!" says he. "The goddam stuff *has* been stole!" Pretty soon the two older brothers come over, and he told 'em what happened.

After while they got him alone for a minute, and Matthew says, "Where did you hide it?" Luke cursed something terrible, and he showed 'em the brush pile and the empty barrel. "You're a-putting on the best act I ever seen, but there ain't no need to keep it up with us," says Mark. "It ain't no act, God damn it!" yells Luke. "The whiskey's gone, I tell you!" His two brothers just looked at him and shook their heads kind of sad. "All right, Luke, if that's the way you want it," says Matthew. So then him and Mark went home and left poor Luke a-hollering and a-quarreling with his wife's kinfolks.

152

About a week after that Luke found a gallon jug of good whiskey on his porch one morning. A couple weeks later there was another gallon, right in the same place. One time when he had company over Sunday there was two jugs on the porch. Luke had figured the whole thing out by this time, and he knowed in reason where the whiskey come from. But he never said one word about it to anybody. Neither did Matthew and Mark. Them boys was awful close-mouthed about things like that.

The Blacksmith's Story

ONE TIME there was a blacksmith that couldn't get no rest of a night, and he kept talking about how he was rode by a witch. Soon as he went to sleep a girl would put a hair bridle on him and ride him all over the country. That's why he was all tired out in the morning. He had scratches on his legs, too, and sometimes there was cockleburs in his hair. If a man was to tell such a tale nowadays folks would think he was crazy, but that was a long time ago, and everybody believed in witches then.

Finally the blacksmith made a dummy and put it in his bed, and then he hid behind the door. When the young witch come in he grabbed the bridle and put it on her. Sure enough, she turned into a fine mare. She bucked and kicked and tried to bite, but the blacksmith stayed right with her. They went a-flying up hills and through briar-patches, and he didn't spare the whip nor spur, neither. The mare didn't have no shoes on,

153

so he went down to the shop. She carried on something terrible, but he tied her up like a ox and shod her all round. Then he snatched off the bridle, and away she run through the timber.

The blacksmith went home and slept fine, and the witch never bothered him no more. But about ten miles away a merchant's daughter showed up missing. Finally they found her, a-hiding in the barn. She was stark naked, with horseshoes nailed to her hands and feet.

There was a lot of talk, but nobody ever done anything about it. Her pappy was a rich merchant and stood in with the county officers. So they just hushed the whole thing up and sent the girl off to a big hospital somewheres. Some of the town folks went so far as to claim it was just one of them old tales, and nothing like that ever did happen nohow.

Mister Sharp and the Old Soldier

ONE TIME there was a bunch of fellows setting in the back end of a little store, and they was telling the God-awfullest windy stories you ever heard. Them fellows took turn about, and it seemed like each one was a bigger liar than the one that come before him. They was all a-trying to see who was the champion.

Finally a fellow named Sharp says that when he lived down by Dutch Mills he seen two wildcats a-fighting in a briar-patch. First one would jump on top of the other, and then the other one would jump on top of *him*. They just took turns a-climbing

154

like that, till naturally both of 'em was plumb off the ground. They kept a-getting higher and higher, and pretty soon they was clear out of sight. So then Mister Sharp rode into town and done his trading. But he says the neighbors come along about two hours later, and they could still hear them bobcats a-yowling and a-spitting away up in the sky. And the folks going to church next morning didn't hear nothing, because the varmints was too high. But they seen wildcat fur a-falling, so they knowed the fight was still going on.

The rest of them windy-spinners just set there awhile, but they couldn't think of no story to match the one Mister Sharp told. It just happened that a old soldier had went around behind the store for a natural reason, and while he was a-standing by the wall he could hear everything Mister Sharp said, but the people in the store didn't know he was there at all. So pretty soon here come the old soldier in the front door, and he says he has been visiting kinfolks down in Logan county. And then he begun to tell how his brother's two boys was a-scuffling on top of Magazine Mountain, and they fell off the bluff accidental.

There wasn't no foolishness about that, because everybody knows old Magazine is the highest mountain in the whole country. So naturally the folks figured them boys was killed, and Mister Sharp says we are all mighty sorry to hear it. But the old soldier just laughed like a fool, and he says they wasn't hurt at all, except maybe a few scratches. "Them boys both fell at the same time," says he, "so they ketched one another in the air, an' saved each other's life."

Everybody just set there with their mouth open for a minute, and Mister Sharp looked like he was going to have a fit. The old soldier took a chew of tobacker, and then he walked out of the store. It's mighty hard to get the best of them old soldiers, when it comes to telling whoppers.

The Boy That Made Up Songs

ONE TIME there was a woman that only had one baby. It was a little boy, and he was pretty near two years old. She was setting beside him, wondering what he would do when he growed up. Just like every woman thinks maybe her boy will be a lawyer or a doctor or a preacher or something. She said a little prayer, and she prayed he would be a great man some day.

All of a sudden the woman heard a tap on the door, and there stood a little stranger. She was one of the good people all right, because she had a regular fairy wand in her hand. There was a little gold thing, like a pen with diamonds on it, hung round her neck. But her clothes was just plain brown, instead of green and other bright colors like the little people are supposed to wear.

The woman asked her to come in and set down. But the little stranger says she is terrible thirsty, as her throat is a-burning up, and could she have a glass of milk? When the milk was poured out she wanted to know is it from a red cow, because if it is from a red cow she can't drink a drop. The woman told her no, because their cow is yellow. So then the little stranger drunk the milk.

Pretty soon she says, "Is your baby a boy or a girl?" and the

156

woman told her it is a boy. She waved her wand over him and says, "Your son will be a great man, and he will make up songs for people to sing all over the country." A minute later the little stranger was gone, and the woman thought maybe she dreamed the whole thing. But there was the glass setting on the stand-table, with a little milk in the bottom of it.

The boy grew up just like other children, only kind of quiet. He didn't have much to say around the house, but sometimes they would find him out in the woods a-talking to himself, and the other kids couldn't make out what he was talking about. By the time he was sixteen that boy didn't do nothing but read books, and his mother wouldn't see him at all for three or four days a-running. Finally he walked off down the road one day, and the folks didn't have no idea what become of him.

They found out after while how he wrote verses and made up songs that people was a-singing all over the country. Everybody thought he was a great man all right, but the folks never seen hide nor hair of him. His mother was pretty old by this time, and she got lonesome. She thought a lot about her boy that had run off to make up songs, and she wished he would come back home. Finally one day he walked right in the door. He told her he was sorry about running off that way, but he had to make up songs, so there wasn't no help for it. The songs was all done now, and he was sick, so he come home to die. Pretty soon he did die sure enough, and the old woman was all alone again.

After the burying was over, the woman thought about it for a long time. And then she says another little prayer. She prayed that the little stranger wouldn't come to anybody else's house and send their boy away to make up songs for people to sing all over the country.

157

It Sure Won't Do No Harm

ONE TIME there was some people up on Sugar Creek had a mighty sick young-un. Her throat was stopped up pretty bad, and she looked feverish, so the folks sent after Doc Holton. When Doc got there he seen old Gram French was ahead of him, but he never let on.

Them granny-women can smell sickness ten mile off, and old Gram French always run over and took charge before the doctor come. And then when Doc got there he'd find the patient a-puking up slippery-elm bark, or maybe all gaumed up with a cow-dung poultice. Doc Holton says Gram French has killed more people than the James boys, but what could he do about it? Gram hated Doc worse'n a rattlesnake, but she always acted nice as pie when he was around. She'd just grin at him and say, "Well, Doctor, these home remedies of mine may not do no good, but they sure won't do no harm."

Mostly Doc never said much, but this time he'd been up all night, and wasn't feeling well nohow. When he found a dirty stinking rag tied round the sick girl's neck it made him pretty mad. "What the hell's this?" says he. Gram just grinned at him, same as always. "Just a old dirty sock, Doctor. The best thing I ever seen for throat sickness. It might not do no good, maybe, but it sure won't do no harm."

Doc didn't return no answer, and he never paid no more attention to Gram till the sick girl was took care of, and he seen she was going to be all right.

158

Pretty soon Gram spoke up again. "I been havin' a misery in my stomach lately, an' catnip tea don't seem to take hold like it used to. What do *you* recommend for such as that, Doctor?"

Doc looked at Gram's tongue and asked her a few questions, and then he says for the girl's mother to fetch him a good big meat-rind, with plenty of fat on it. "My goodness, Doctor," says Gram, "I never heard tell of usin' a meat-rind for stomach trouble in all my sixty years of nursin' the sick!"

When the woman come back with the meat-rind, Doc passed it over to Gram. "Tie this on your old rump," says he, "and leave it there till it stinks as bad as this dirty sock. It may not do no good," he says, "but it sure won't do you no harm."

The old granny just set there plumb flabbergasted, and Doc throwed the dirty sock in the fire, a-washing his hands careful with stuff out of a bottle. He looked mighty pleased about something. But they do say that Gram French never spoke another word to Doc Holton as long as she lived.

Rena Killed a Stranger

ONE TIME there was a girl named Irene, but everybody called her Rena. She was a good girl and a pretty girl, and the folks thought a lot of her. She went over to her grandmaw's house one time, and a stranger come to the door. Some kind of a salesman, it looked like. He says he wanted a drink. Rena knowed he was a Yankee the minute he opened his mouth, but she give him a gourd of buttermilk anyhow.

159

Soon as he drunk the buttermilk the fellow says maybe you got some whiskey, as I hear everybody down here is moonshiners. Rena told him this is my grandmaw's house, and Grandmaw ain't no moonshiner. Then she says, "Stranger, I think you better go back to town." But the Yankee just laughed, and he grabbed Rena round the middle. Grandmaw jumped up, and the fellow turned Rena loose and slapped the old woman's face. That's where he made a bad mistake, because Rena snatched up the poker and knocked him flat.

Two of old man Clark's boys come along just then, and Rena hollered them into the house. The stranger had got up on his feet by that time, but he looked kind of glassy-eyed, and he didn't say nothing. "This fellow has been drinkin' too much," says Rena. "Will you boys please take him back to town?" The boys was looking at Granny, and one of 'em says, "Don't you reckon we better throw the skunk in the river?" But Rena says, "No, I don't want you to hurt a hair of his head. This man was raised up North somewhere, and we got to make allowances. He just don't know how to behave amongst folks like us." And she made them promise to see that the fellow got safe back to the hotel.

All this time the stranger never said one word, and he still looked glassy-eyed. The boys took a-hold of his arms and started for town, but they wasn't hardly out of sight till he fell right down in the road. And when the boys went to pick him up they seen he was dead. "Well," says one of the boys, "it looks like Rena has done killed herself a peddler." And the other one says, "Yes, but if she finds it out Rena will feel terrible, because she don't believe in killin' people." So pretty soon the boys dragged the dead man over behind some bushes.

"It won't do to tell the sheriff," says one, "because Rena would hear about it. And if Doc examines the corpse, he'll know it was a crack on the head that killed him." And the other one says, "Rena will find out she has killed a man, or else she will think we done it. And it's a bad business either way." So finally they decided to get a pick and shovel and bury the Yankee under the bluff, and not say nothing to nobody. So that's what they done.

Well, sir, Rena is an old lady now, with grandchildren all over the place. No better woman ever lived, and she's been a shining light in this community for more than sixty years. If Rena knowed she killed that fellow, it might have soured her some way, and maybe ruined her whole life. So it looks like them Clark boys done the right thing, law or no law. What do *you* think about it?

Devil Take the Skillet

ONE TIME an old fellow was camped on Sugar Creek, a-trying to cook him a mess of fish. He built his little fire under a ledge, because it was a-raining. The wood all got wet, and there wasn't enough grease, and the fryin' pan broke so the handle had to be wired on. The old man was pretty hungry, and smoke got in his eyes, and it seemed like everything went wrong. Finally the handle on the skillet come loose, and most of his grease spilled out in the fire. The old fellow belonged to the Pentecostal Church that don't believe in cussing, but when the handle slipped he says, "Devil take it!" Just then

161

he looked up, and there stood the Devil a-grinning through the smoke.

The Devil didn't speak no regular words, but he growled like a big dog and swung his tail around. There was three sharp prongs on the end of the tail. Then he opened his mouth big as a bear trap and walked right through the fire. The old man was scared pretty near to death, but he stood up with the fryin' pan in his hand. All of a sudden he throwed pan, grease, fish, and all right into the Devil's mouth.

Old Scratch yelled so loud it shook the whole country, and blowed sparks fifty foot high, and tore down saplings all the way to the creek. When he hit the water the steam misted up the whole valley like a July fog. The old man was down on his knees a-praying by this time, and the Devil went plumb out of sight. The skillet was gone too, and nobody ever did find it.

When the old man told the folks what happened, most of them just kind of snickered, because they figured the old fellow must have dreamed it. But he showed 'em something that stopped their giggling mighty sudden. About twenty foot back from the fire stood a ironwood tree, and there was a kind of horn stuck plumb through it. The thing was thin and black, sharp on both sides like a double-edged knife. It was pretty near two foot long. The folks looked at the horn mighty close, but nary one of 'em touched it.

The old man swore it was one of the prongs off the Devil's tail, and maybe it was. There ain't no animal in this country has got such a horn as that. Like the old man says, if it didn't come off'n the Devil's tail, where did it come from?

162

The Hog-Bristle Trial

ONE TIME old Deacon Jones come riding into town, and he says young Johnny Benton has beat him up something terrible. The doctor looked the deacon over, and he says both eyes is blacked and his nose seems to be broke, also somebody has been a-stomping him in the mud, so maybe he is injured internal. "An' that ain't all," says the deacon. "The young hellion pulled out a handful of my beard and throwed it in my face!" And with that he showed the sheriff a bunch of hair he'd picked up after the fight was over.

The sheriff went out to arrest Johnny Benton, and the prosecuting attorney sealed the deacon's whiskers in a envelope and put it in the safe. When Johnny's trial come up the deacon told how the defendant beat him pretty near to death without no reason at all, and then he says this young ruffian pulled my whiskers out by the roots. So now the prosecuting attorney has got the whiskers in a envelope, and it is called Exhibit A. But when they passed Exhibit A to the jury them fellows busted out laughing, because Exhibit A was nothing but bristles out of a brown hog. The bristles was exactly the color of Deacon Jones's beard, but they was hog-bristles just the same.

Finally the Judge put on his specs and looked very careful, and he didn't say nothing but you could see that he knowed they was hog-bristles. And Johnny's lawyer says you might fool city jurymen with such a trick, but the intelligent gentlemen of this jury are farmers and stock raisers, and they know hog-bristles when they see 'em. The prosecuting attorney begun to holler that the evidence has been tampered with, and he says if you let that pettifogger get by with it we might as well tear down the courthouse and eat our meat raw, because there ain't no law nor justice in this county, he says. And so the judge made him shut up, or else he would be fined for contempt of court.

Pretty soon the jury turned in a verdict of "Not Guilty," so Johnny Benton was a free man, and Johnny's lawyer just set there a-grinning at the prosecuting attorney. But everybody knowed in reason that the prosecuting attorney sealed up the deacon's whiskers in the envelope. Somebody must have switched envelopes, but the prosecutor couldn't figure out how they done it.

Most folks thought that Johnny's lawyer knowed more about it than anybody else, but he never let on. Him and the prosecuting attorney are both dead now. But some of the old-timers are still a-wrangling about what happened at Johnny Benton's trial.

Too Much Church Work

ONE TIME there was a young doctor come to our settlement, and he was just out of medical school. He got an old doctor to show him around the neighborhood for a few days, so he could get acquainted with the folks and see what kind of doctoring they was used to.

The first house they stopped at, the old doctor felt a sick

woman's pulse. "You've been eating too much sweet stuff," says he. Then he give the woman some pills, and that's all there was to it. When they got back in the buggy the young doctor says, "You didn't examine that woman. How did you know what was the matter with her?" The old doctor just grinned. "Didn't you see all those candy-bar wrappings in the fireplace?" says he.

When they come to the next house, the old doctor felt a sick man's pulse and looked at his tongue. "You've been smoking too much," says he. Then he left some pills on the table, and that's all there was to it. "You didn't give that fellow any examination, either," says the young doctor. "How did you know what was wrong with him?" The old doctor just grinned. "Didn't you see those cigaret butts all over the floor?" he says.

On their way to the next house, the old doctor says, "The woman that lives here is a grass-widow, and she is pretty sick. Suppose you take this case, and we'll see how you make out." So the young doctor felt the woman's pulse and looked at her tongue. "You've been doing too much church work," he says, "and I advise you to go easy for awhile." Then he give her some pills, and that's all there was to it.

When they got back in the buggy the old doctor says, "Too much religion is driving that woman crazy. I told her so, years ago. But you never saw the patient before. How on earth did *you* know what is the matter with her?" The young doctor just grinned. "Didn't you see that preacher under the bed?" says he.

165

The Stolen Wedges

ONE TIME there was a preacher named Lorenzo Dow, and he held big camp meetings all over the country. An old-timer kept complaining about how somebody has stole his iron wedges, that they used to split rails with. Preacher Dow says never mind, just give me a wedge like the ones you lost, and I will find out who is the thief.

So that night, right in the middle of the meeting, old Dow had 'em all shouting and praying. All of a sudden he pulled out a big old iron wedge, and waved it over the pulpit like he was going to throw it. "May God carry this straight to the head of the man that stole Brother Ralston's wedges!" he yelled.

Mostly the people just looked kind of surprised, but a fellow in the second row ducked. "That's the guilty man!" says Preacher Dow. So then everybody begun to sing and pray louder than ever. The thief confessed right there, and got religion, and gave the wedges back, and begged everybody to forgive him. Some of them old-time preachers was awful handy when it come to things like that.

Babes in the Woods

ONE TIME there was a man and his wife took two orphans to raise. But the kids kept a-crying of a night, so the woman says let's cut their throats and put 'em out of their misery. The man says he don't believe in cutting children's throats, and it is better just to leave them out in the woods somewheres. If they get lost accidental it ain't our fault, he says, and maybe the bears will eat 'em up.

So they took the children away out in the mountains, and told them it was to pick huckleberries. And when night come

167

they was all alone, and the little girl begun to cry. Pretty soon the little boy begun to cry too, because they was hungry and scared. So then they both laid down on the ground and piled leaves on each other to keep warm.

Along in the night the big brown bears come, and they was a-looking for something to eat. The bears come a-snuffing and a-snoofing in the dry leaves. Pretty soon they found the little girl and gobbled her right up. The little boy run away, and you could hear him a-hollering. But the big brown bears ketched him, and they gobbled him up, too. So then you couldn't hear nothing but them big bears a-snoofing and a-snuffing in the dry leaves. And that's all there is to the story.

Notes

IN the following notes, "Motif" and "Type" refer to *Motif-Index of Folk-Literature* by Stith Thompson and *The Types of the Folk-Tale* by Antti Aarne and Stith Thompson. These two books contain keys to published European folklore collections, as well as to the indices of folk tales in the European folklore archives.

THE DEVIL'S PRETTY DAUGHTER

Told by Mrs. Marie Wilbur, Pineville, Mo., June, 1930. She had it from Mrs. Lucinda Mosier, also of Pineville, who heard the story from her elders in the late 1870's. Cf. *Midwest Folklore*, II (Summer, 1952), 77–79. (V.R.)

This is a version of Type 313, "The Girl as Helper in the Hero's Flight." The magic flight obstacles in this Ozark text are beautifully localized by the unusual introduction of folk beliefs to re-enforce the obstacles; e.g., the running water which the Devil cannot cross, and the paper with holy words which he, of course, cannot stand. Chase (*Jack Tales*, pp. 135–50) gives a Virginia version, for which I furnished references (on p. 198) to American, Scottish, and Irish versions. To those notes should be added: Johnson, *Folk Culture on St. Helena Island, South Carolina*, pp. 150–51 (Negro); Carrière, *Tales from the French Folk-Lore of Missouri*, pp. 81–83; Claudel, *Southern Folklore Quarterly*, IX, 191–208 (English translations of several Louisiana French texts plus one from France, and some discussion); Claudel, *Journal of American Folklore*, LVIII, 210–12 (Louisiana; Spanish); Aiken, *Publications of the Texas Folklore Society*, XII, 61–66 (from Texas Mexicans); MacManus, *Donegal Wonder Book*, pp. 251–84 (Ireland); Curtin, *Irish Folk-Tales*, edited by S. O'Duilearga (Dublin, 1943), pp. 25–34, with excel-

169

lent references on pp. 159–60. See also Parsons, *Antilles,* III, 153 ff., for excellent references and abstracts of 22 tales. The motif of the magical obstacles in the flight is combined with the dog helpers' story in a curious *cante fable* from North Carolina in Wright, *Journal of American Folklore,* LIV, 197–99.

The magic flight, but with an animal helper, is also found in Type 314, "The Youth Transformed into a Horse." See: Claudel, *Southern Folklore Quarterly,* V, 257–63 (Louisiana; French); Mac-Manus, *Donegal Fairy Stories,* pp. 97–131 (Ireland). (H.H.)

WHAT CANDY ASHCRAFT DONE

Told by Mr. John Chaney, Springfield, Mo., October, 1945. He credited the tale to his mother's people, who lived in Howell county, Mo., and Boone county, Ark., in the early days. (V.R.)

Motif K 311.1, "Thief disguised as corpse"; Type 966.* Boggs (*Journal of American Folklore,* XLVII, 319) gives a North Carolina form of this yarn in which the woman's husband is not at home and the pretended corpse is a man. The wife shoots one of the men and traps the other in a shallow well, keeping him there till her husband returns home. In related versions of this legend from northern England and Scotland summarized by Bett (*English Legends,* p. 42), a robber disguised as a peddler is refused lodging for the night, but gets permission to leave his "long pack" in the house overnight. A shot through the pack kills his accomplice who is hidden in it, effectually preventing him from opening the house door during the night. British versions of this legend were probably affected by James Hogg's "The Long Pack; a Northumbrian Tale," which was popular in chapbooks issued by many publishers. See Harry B. Weiss, *A Book about Chapbooks* (Trenton, N.J., 1942), p. 51. (H.H.)

A SLIM YELLOW CATFISH

Told by Dr. Leo McKellops, Anderson, Mo., May, 1933. He heard it near Steelville, Mo., in the early 1900's. "My neighbors recounted this as a recent happening," said McKellops, "but I think it's an old Irish fairy-story."

170

Several related stories are known in the Ozark region. Robert L. Morris, of the University of Arkansas (*Folk-Say*, 1931, pp. 97–98), has one about a fish which turned into a woman. E. A. Collins (*Folk Tales of Missouri*, 1935, pp. 113–14) tells of a woman who became an eel. As recently as 1920, Mr. Price Paine of Noel, Mo., met old-timers who believed that a man had been somehow transformed into a catfish. Cf. my *We Always Lie to Strangers* (1951, p. 162), also *Fantasy and Science Fiction* (November, 1952, pp. 116–17). (V.R.)

This story, and the others referred to by Mr. Randolph, are the only examples I can find in the Anglo-American tradition of the theme listed as Motif B 81.2, "Mermaid marries man." There are, however, Welsh legends in which a mortal marries a water lady, in W. Sikes, *British Goblins* (Boston, 1881), pp. 38–44. Since the fish lady is from fresh water, see also Motif F 420.1.2, "Water-spirit as woman," and F 420.1.6.7, "Water-spirits are nude." The theme of the supernatural woman who doffs her bird, animal, or mermaid form, becomes human, lives with a man, and later leaves him comes under Type 400, "The Man on a Quest for His Lost Wife." See the study of "Swan-Maidens," by E. S. Hartland, *The Science of Fairy Tales* (2nd ed., London, 1925), pp. 255–332. Much closer to the Ozark version is a South Wales legend given by Hartland (*Folk-Lore*, XVI, 337–39). A boy catches a salmon which turns into a naked girl. She overcomes his reluctance to become her lover first by almost drowning him, then by kissing him so vigorously that he tastes the blood from her cut lip. He loves her passionately all his life and they have many children. (H.H.)

OLD WALL-EYES

Told by Mr. Ray Wood, Houston, Texas, March, 1951. Wood collected many songs and stories in the Ozarks. He used to edit a folklore column, "That Ain't the Way I Heard It," in the *Times-Record* at Fort Smith, Ark., and is the author of a fine book entitled *Mother Goose in the Ozarks* (Raywood, Texas, 1938, 58 pp.).

Many elderly persons in the Ozarks know this tale, in several

171

versions. Some of them call the monster "Old Whirl-Eyes," others say that his proper title is "Raw Meat and Bloody Bones." (V.R.)

Both in England and America there are references (rather than stories) to many mythical monsters, some of which are apparently derived from local demons or boggarts. Such terrifying figures are chiefly used to frighten children. The best known of these is "Raw Head and Bloody Bones." See: Charles Hardwick, *Traditions, Superstitions, and Folklore: Chiefly Lancashire and the North of England* (Manchester and London, 1872), p. 131; John Brand, *Observations on the Popular Antiquities of Great Britain* (London, 1849), II, 516. Brand quotes Samuel Butler's *Hudibras* as a seventeenth-century reference; Butler, however, speaks of not one but two figures—"Raw Heads" and "Bloody-bones."

Pursuit by a meat-eating "Thing" is found in a Tennessee story given by Anderson, *Tennessee Folklore Society Bulletin*, V, 55–57, reprinted in Botkin, *A Treasury of Southern Folklore*, pp. 517–18; retold in Vincent, *Bert Vincent's Strolling*, pp. [35]–[37]. In the Anderson version a rabbit tricks the "Thing" into killing itself. Except for its ending, Mr. Randolph's story resembles the classic legend of the man in a wagon or sled who delays pursuing wolves by throwing them meat or fish. See Federal Writers' Project of the Work Projects Administration, *Idaho Lore*, p. 94 (hogs); Gore and Speare, *New Hampshire Folk Tales*, pp. 108–9 (fish). (H.H.)

THE CUCKOO'S NEST

Told by Mr. Lew Beardon, Branson, Mo., December, 1938. He had it from an old woman who lived on Bear Creek, in Taney county, Mo. I believe that Mr. Beardon, or his informant, changed the horse-trader's song so as to eliminate some "unprintable" words. (V.R.)

The Ozark text is the fifth version of this *cante fable* to be reported from America. About the same number of texts have been published in Great Britain. The piece is related to an old European song, "Mîn mann is to hûs." I published several New Jersey variants and full notes in the *Journal of American Folklore*, LV, 137–

172

40. In this Ozark version, as in those from New Jersey and North Carolina, the husband understands his wife's song to her lover and substitutes his own stanza. (H.H.)

AUNT KATE'S GOOMER-DUST

Told by Mr. J. H. Storey, Pineville, Mo., July, 1922. Mr. Storey heard the tale in the 1870's or early 1880's, at his old home near Pea Ridge, Ark. (V.R.)

Chaucer would have enjoyed a story like this, but most British and American scholars apparently feel timid about the earthiness of such yarns and there are few parallels in the published literature. In a closely related North Carolina story given by Boggs (*Journal of American Folklore*, XLVII, 320), the rejected lover puts a "horsehair witchball" under his girl's doorstep. All who cross the doorstep—the girl, her parents, even the doctor who comes to cure them—"poop" with every word they say. The parents are forced to consent to the wedding, and the witchball is quietly removed. These American texts seem to be versions of Type 593, "Fiddevav." In an Irish version (*Handbook of Irish Folklore*, p. 569) the hidden magic object makes all who poke in the fire sneeze, cough, or belch incessantly until the object is removed. (H.H.)

THE BABY IN THE CRADLE

Told by Mrs. Ethel Thompson, Hot Springs, Ark., April, 1938. She had it from some country folk who came to the Public Library. Mrs. Thompson thought it was probably a true story.

Allsopp (*Folklore of Romantic Arkansas*, 1931, II, 174–75) relates a slightly different version which he had from Mrs. Sam H. Wassell, of Little Rock, Ark., in 1919. Senator Tom Heflin told the same yarn in the United States Senate, April 26, 1932, representing the central character as "an old Negro down in Arkansas" (*Record of the 72nd Congress*, p. 8942). Heflin's tale is reprinted in *Journal of American Folklore*, XLVII (1934), 379. (V.R.)

This tale is a version of Motif K 406.2, "Stolen sheep dressed as baby in cradle." American texts speak of a hog in the cradle. The apparent substitution of one animal for another might be explained

173

by the fact that in some English dialects the word "hog" means a sheep or young lamb. Versions of this tale have interested students of medieval English literature because of their resemblance to a humorous incident in the *Secunda Pastorum* (Second Shepherd's Play) in the Townley Cycle. In it Mak steals a lamb, puts it in a cradle, and has his wife lie in "childbed." When the owners come demanding the lamb, he is singing the "child" a lullaby. He invites them to search the house, but quietly, since his wife is ill. When the fraud is discovered, Mak and his wife insist she has borne the "child," but that it has been bewitched. After a careful study, Cosbey (*Speculum,* XX, 310–17) concludes that the playwright was using a contemporary folk tale. In his examination of twelve texts, Cosbey considers only four American versions: that by Heflin (referred to above) which the Alabama senator told the Senate on at least three occasions; a Georgia version printed by Stroup (*Southern Folklore Quarterly,* III, 5–6); a North Carolina version, also from Stroup (*Journal of American Folklore,* XLVII, 380–81); and a southern folk song version. Stroup pointed out that the Heflin version was spread over the country in Will Rogers's syndicated column. The Ozark version and a Texas Negro variant printed by Brewer (*Publications of the Texas Folklore Society,* X, 12–13) are close to the Heflin form; in these the thief pretends the child is very ill. A South Carolina Negro text given by Parsons (*Journal of American Folklore,* XXXIV, 20) resembles these but lacks the cradle episode. The Allsopp text referred to by Mr. Randolph also has the "sick child" in the cradle, but when it is uncovered the old Negro and his wife pretend the child was bewitched, and begin to pray for it. This resembles the Mak story. (H.H.)

SETTING DOWN THE BUDGET

Told by Mr. T. A. McQuary, Galena, Mo., December, 1935. "It's just an old fable, like people used to tell their children," he said. "I heard it down in Arkansas, when I was a young man."

Press Woodruff (*A Backwoods Philosopher from Arkansaw,* 1901, pp. 267–71) prints a fantastic variant of this tale entitled "The Contented Man." According to Woodruff's story, it is a red calf that runs up the tree, a horse that eats the meat, a mule that steals the cornmeal, and a girl who forces the man off the footlog into the water. (V.R.)

The theme of accepting with contentment a series of worsening changes of fortune is also found in a story from Nova Scotia given by Fauset (*Folklore from Nova Scotia,* pp. 105–6); and in one from Northumberland, England, given by Jacobs (*More English Fairy Tales,* pp. 50–53; No. 53). In these the changes begin with the discovery of a pot of gold which transforms itself rapidly into almost nothing. The story seems distantly related to Type 1415, "Lucky Hans," in which the man starts with something of great value, stupidly swaps it each time for something of less value, yet seems contented each time with his bad bargain. (H.H.)

THE SOOT ON SOMEBODY'S BACK

Told by Mrs. Marie Wilbur, Pineville, Mo., May, 1930. She had the story from an old woman in McDonald county, Mo., who regarded it as the truth. (V.R.)

This is a version of Motif H 58, "Telltale hand-mark." This recognition motif is found in European and Asiatic tales and among the American Indians, but I believe this is the first report of this story from American-white narrators. In some versions the sister's discovery of her brother's guilt has as its sequel that she becomes the sun, he the moon—and he continues to pursue her (Motif A 736.1, "Sun sister and moon brother"), as in the version from northern Idaho Indians given in Federal Writers' Project of the Work Projects Administration, *Idaho Lore,* p. 150. (H.H.)

GRAVE ROBBERS

Told by Mr. A. B. Macdonald, Kansas City, Mo., May, 1933. He said that it was known to many old-timers in Jackson county, Mo. Macdonald was a reporter on the Kansas City *Star,* and thought that the story had appeared in one of the Kansas City papers, but we were unable to find it in the files.

I published a short version of this tale in *Ozark Ghost Stories* (1944, p. 5), and it was reprinted in my *Ozark Superstitions* (1947,

175

p. 214). Since 1944 I have heard several different versions from Kansas City and Independence, Mo. Old residents tell me that something of the sort really occurred in the 1880's, and that accounts of the incident were printed in Missouri newspapers. Cf. *Southern Folklore Quarterly,* XVI (1952), 171–72. (V.R.)

In a version from Iowa given by Musick (*Hoosier Folklore,* V, 106), a man substitutes himself for the corpse which had been rolled in a blanket, and is lifted to the buggy seat between the two robbers. When offered a drink, he accepts and stretches out his hand, scaring the men away.

In a Virginia Negro text in Bacon and Parsons (*Journal of American Folklore,* XXXV, 300–301), a trickster crawls into the grave robber's wagon. When the grave robber, who has been drinking, feels the hand of the supposed corpse, he says to his partner, "This fellow's hand is hot." The trickster says, "If you had been in hell as long as I have, your hands would be hot too."

In a New England version in Botkin (*A Treasury of New England Folklore,* p. 95), a watchman hides under the white sheet over the coffin that the grave robbers are about to carry away. One of them complains about the weight of the body; whereupon the hidden trickster frightens them by saying that if he is too heavy, he can walk.

A Scottish chapbook reprinted by Cunningham (*Amusing Prose Chap-Books,* p. 218), tells of a poor boy who has to sleep in the churchyard at Falkirk. Hearing two "resurrection men" arguing about how to secure the horse they have along to carry the corpse, the lad creeps out and offers to hold the beast. The men flee— leaving the horse. (H.H.)

ROUND THE CAMPFIRE

Told by Mr. H. F. Walker, Joplin, Mo., September, 1923. Walker had it from an "Oklahoma hillbilly" who worked in the Kansas City Southern shops at Pittsburg, Kan., just across the Missouri-Kansas border.

This is a circular or "teaser" story, perhaps a children's bedtime tale like "The Locusts Got the Corn." I heard a similar yarn at

176

Fort Smith, Ark., in 1944, with the word "bastard" used instead of "cowpuncher." (V.R.)

This belongs to Type 2350, "Rounds. Stories which begin over and over again and repeat," in the revision of the formula tale section of the Aarne-Thompson index by Taylor (*Journal of American Folklore,* XLVI, 88). The characters sitting around the campfire differ in the various American texts. See: Halpert and others, *Hoosier Folklore Bulletin,* I, 88–89 (Indiana; boys; Big John and Little John); Stimson, *Journal of American Folklore,* LVIII, 129 (New York City; brigands); Carl Withers, *A Rocket in My Pocket* (New York, 1948), p. 131 (from Brooklyn College students; Indians); Hoffman, *New York Folklore Quarterly,* IV, 209 (New York; a captain and his men); Lanctôt, *Journal of American Folklore,* XXIX, 50 (Canadian French; brigands). Two unpublished versions from Kentucky in the Halpert collections have some differences: a captain and lieutenant sit on a log (Hopkins county); three robbers in a cave (Graves county). (H.H.)

YELLOW BREAD

Told by Mrs. Pearl Spurlock, Branson, Mo. The date is missing from my record, but it must have been in the Winter of 1934 or the Spring of 1935.

Mr. J. C. Edwards, Webster Groves, Mo., October, 1950, has an almost identical tale which he heard in rural Missouri about 1890. (V.R.)

Atkinson and Dobie, who give a pioneer Texas version of this yarn (*Publications of the Texas Folklore Society,* VII, 69–70, and reprinted in both Botkin, *A Treasury of American Folklore,* pp. 412–13, and Boatright, *Folk Laughter on the American Frontier,* pp. 52–53), suggest that such a story was told in pioneer days to teach children manners and inform them of the elegancies of civilization that had been left behind. In the Ozarks and Texas the ignorant man thinks the cake is cornbread. Boatright (p. 53, n.) says it is angel food cake in some Texas versions and the speech is, "This here light bread is good enough for me." In a Nova Scotia text by Creighton (*Folklore of Lunenberg County, Nova Scotia,*

177

p. 128), the ignorant man makes inroads in a dark fruitcake, and refuses other food saying, "This brown bread's good enough for me." (H.H.)

FALSE FACES IN MISSOURI

Told by a gentleman who wishes to remain anonymous, Fayetteville, Ark., June, 1950. He had the story from friends in Joplin, Mo.

I have never seen this yarn in print, but it was widely known in the middle 1940's, perhaps earlier. In November, 1947, a salesman from Springfield, Mo., assured me that it was a true story; he believed that the hero of the tale was "Spider" Rowland of Little Rock, who used to do a column for the *Arkansas Gazette.* (V.R.)

THE PEDDLER WANTED FISH

Told by Mr. Charles S. Hiatt, Cassville, Mo., April, 1933. He says that it actually happened at the Ben Irwin Hotel, in Cassville.

Compare the account in my pamphlet *Funny Stories about Hillbillies* (1944, p. 22). The hotel mentioned by Mr. Hiatt was a landmark for many years, known all over southwest Missouri. Mr. and Mrs. Ben Irwin were still running the place as recently as October, 1950. See Homer Croy (*What Grandpa Laughed At,* 1948, p. 241) for a related tale about something that happened near Maryville, Mo. (V.R.)

A similar goldfish-eating story is given in *Folk-Lore Sketches and Reminiscences of New Hampshire Life,* by the Folk-Lore Committee, New Hampshire's Daughters, but I have mislaid the page reference. (H.H.)

SPANISH GOLD

Told by Mr. H. F. Walker, Joplin, Mo., July, 1923. He had it from an old-timer at Sulphur Springs, Ark.

The Ozark country is full of yarns about buried gold. I am personally acquainted with men who spent years in the search for this legendary treasure. The business of Spaniards and Indians and buckskin maps is part of the "Lost Louisiana" tale known all over the Southwest. See my *The Ozarks* (1931, pp. 277–98).

W. A. Dorrance (*Three Ozark Streams,* 1937, p. 45) tells the story of Jake Hepburn, who lived on the Current River in Carter county, Mo. When Jake started to search a cavern for buried gold he was stopped by something like an earthquake. "They'se some folks that *kain't* dig for treasure," a native explained to Dorrance. (V.R.)

BESSIE AND THE EGGS

Told by Miss Marion Neville, Chesterton, Ind., November, 1950. She heard the story from a girl in Springfield, Mo., about 1912. Most of the cyclone stories in this part of Missouri derive from the "Marshfield Tornado" which did a lot of damage in 1880. (V.R.)

HORN EATS HORN

Told by Mr. Bob Wyrick, Eureka Springs, Ark., November, 1950. He heard it near Green Forest, Ark., about 1900. "People must have been kind of crazy about riddles, in the olden times," he said. "It's funny a man would be eatin' horn, though. Must have better teeth than I got."

The riddle in this tale is well known, but the man's name is usually Corn, not Horn. In most Ozark versions he is a Confederate soldier who ate parched corn in a treetop where he was hiding from bushwhackers. Compare *Journal of American Folklore,* XLVII (1934), 86 and *Southern Folklore Quarterly,* VIII (1944), 9. Also *Ozark Folklore* (I, No. 3 [May 30, 1951], 5), a mimeographed bulletin issued at the University of Arkansas. For further information about this type of riddle, see Halpert (*Southern Folklore Quarterly,* V [1941], 197–200). (V.R.)

This is one of the riddle-tales discussed in the excellent article by F. J. Norton, "Prisoner Who Saved His Neck With a Riddle," *Folk-Lore,* LIII, 27–57. I am assembling American references to this riddle-tale to annotate several texts in the Halpert collections. (H.H.)

A HUNTER CALLS HIS SHOTS

Told by Dr. Glenn Jones, Crane, Mo., July, 1939. Some of the local sportsmen thought that Jones himself was the central figure.

But he said it was the experience of a salesman from Kansas City, who came to Taney county, Mo., about 1914.

In November, 1950, it occurred to me to check the facts in this story. I opened a Remington-UMC "Sureshot" 12-gauge shell, loaded with 3½ drams of powder and 1⅛ ounces of No. 5 shot, and counted the pellets. My figure was 199, which is close enough. (V.R.)

ANDY COGGBURN'S SONG

Told by Mr. W. T. Moore, Taney county, Mo., November, 1939. Mr. Moore saw these outlaws in action and knew many of them personally.

The Bald Knobbers were vigilantes who operated in Taney and Christian counties, Mo., in the 1880's. The best book about these people is *Bald Knobbers* (1939, 253 pp.) by Lucile Morris of Springfield, Mo. "Cap" Kinney was an ex-bartender who killed Andrew Coggburn at the Oak Grove schoolhouse, not far from Branson, Mo., March 12, 1886. Sam Snapp was murdered by Wash Middleton at Kirbyville, Mo., May 9, 1886. Kinney was shot to death in Forsyth, Mo., Aug. 20, 1888. Several versions of the Coggburn song, with some information about its provenience, are printed in my *Ozark Folksongs* (II, 1948, 114–17). (V.R.)

THE DUMB-BULL

Told by Mr. Willie Lewis, Galena, Mo., March, 1943. He had heard the tale from several James River guides. When I interviewed these men, they declared that it was a true story.

Panthers are rare in the Ozarks now, though one was killed near Hot Springs, Ark., in December, 1949 (*Arkansas Gazette,* Dec. 3, 1949). But "panther scares" are still common all over Missouri and Arkansas; they had one in Barry county, Mo., early in 1950 (Galena, Mo., *News-Oracle,* Feb. 15, 1950). The dumb-bull joke is well known; I have seen several dumb-bulls, and helped to make one; it sounded rather like a sea lion, but much louder. It is said that Mr. Clifford Palmer, Walnut Shade, Mo., built a gigantic dumb-bull that frightened people all over Taney county in the middle 1930's. Compare May Kennedy McCord (Springfield, Mo., *News and Leader,* Nov. 8, 1936). (V.R.)

In a report in the Halpert collections the unwilling hosts of a lazy, dirty, cowardly man in Caldwell county, Kentucky, place a "dumb-bull" in his room and work it after he has fallen asleep. He is thoroughly frightened. The joke backfires, however, because he keeps his hosts awake the rest of the night. (H.H.)

GUNPOWDER IN THE STOVE

Told by Mr. A. L. Cline, Joplin, Mo., July, 1922. He heard it as a true story in Benton county, Ark., about 1895.

This yarn is known all through the Ozark country, with local names and definite locations. Mr. Clarence Sharp, Pittsburg, Kan., told me that he heard it as a boy at Dutch Mills, Ark., in the 1890's. Three times, in different parts of south Missouri and northwest Arkansas, citizens have pointed out to me the identical store building where the incident occurred. Compare my pamphlet *Funny Stories about Hillbillies* (1944, p. 22). (V.R.)

The title story in Jagendorf (*Sand in the Bag,* pp. 135–37) gives a southern Illinois version of this trick for ridding a store of loafers. The storekeeper's friend comes into the store with a tied-up bundle of gunpowder and asks for shot on credit. When this is refused, he loses his temper and says if he can't get shot he doesn't need gunpowder—and throws the bundle (which contains only sand) into the hot stove. The loafers flee.

The basic theme of this story—pretending to put an explosive in a hot stove—is found in a cowboy story told by Thorp (*Tales of the Chuck Wagon,* pp. 118–23; reprinted with some changes in Thorp and Clark, *Pardner of the Wind,* pp. 217–19). A cowboy, refused for the sixtieth time by a supercilious schoolmarm, says, "We will die together," and pretends to put live cartridges in the stove. The lady jumps out of the window to escape, losing most of her clothes en route.

A similar device is found in a story about two army officers told by Brown (*Wit and Humor,* pp. 237–38). A lieutenant revenges himself on a boastful captain by placing a gunpowder canister in

181

the center of the fire in the captain's quarters, then runs out and locks the captain inside. The latter jumps through the window in his underclothes—only to be told there was no powder in the canister. One of my students copied a story for me from an unpublished manuscript history of McLemoresville, Tennessee, written by Professor E. H. Harrell. Shortly after the Civil War a tramp entered a McLemoresville saloon, asked for a drink, and was refused. He left, wrapped a brickbat in paper, then returned and repeated his request. When the saloonkeeper told him to go to hell, he retorted, "All right, we'll just go to hell together," and threw his package into the fire. The saloonkeeper, thinking the package contained gunpowder, leaped over the bar and fled. The tramp calmly went behind the bar and helped himself. (H.H.)

SLIPPING THROUGH THE KEYHOLE

Told by Mr. John Chaney, Springfield, Mo., October, 1945. He had it from his mother's people, who lived in Howell county, Mo., in the 1870's.

Many hillfolk know this tale, in several versions. I referred to it briefly in *Ozark Superstitions* (1947, pp. 273–74). Compare *Midwest Folklore,* II (Summer, 1952), 79–80; also *Fantasy and Science Fiction,* IV, No. 2 (February, 1953), 75–76. (V.R.)

The story of the boy who imitates witches and joins in their travels is very popular, both in America and Europe, yet is strangely absent from the Aarne-Thompson type index. In typical forms of the tale, the boy imitates the witches, rubs on a salve, repeats a verbal formula, flies out through the chimney, and joins the witches in a dance. Often he puts on a magic cap, or rides some object or animal that furnishes him with aerial transportation. Sometimes something occurs (e.g., he breaks the charm by speaking) and he is left miles from the place where he started. At other times he follows the witches into a store or a cellar, but then is left behind, caught by the owner, and often sentenced to death by hanging. While he is on the scaffold, one of the witches brings him the magic cap, and he escapes by putting it on and repeating the verbal charm.

182

American Negro versions are sometimes combined with the story of the witch who removes her skin, which is then filled with salt and pepper so that she cannot put it on again. See Parsons, *Antilles,* III, 149–50, for references to the latter story.

For the witch-imitator see Gardner, *Folklore from the Schoharie Hills, New York,* pp. 62–64 (with good references; text reprinted from *Journal of American Folklore,* XXVII, 306–7); Reynard, *The Narrow Land,* pp. 156–58 (Massachusetts); Brendle and Troxell, *Pennsylvania German Folk Tales,* pp. 147–48; Whitney and Bullock, *Folk-Lore from Maryland,* pp. 197–98 (two Negro texts reprinted from *Journal of American Folklore:* the first from Seip, *ibid.,* XIV, 40–41; the second from Bergen, *ibid.,* XII, 68); Parsons, *Journal of American Folklore,* XXX, 209–10 (Maryland; Negro); *ibid.,* 187–88 (North Carolina; Negro); Bacon and Parsons, *ibid.,* XXXV, 286–87 and notes (Virginia; Negro); Cross, *ibid.,* XXII, 251 (North Carolina: Negro); *ibid.,* 254 (North Carolina; White); Parsons, *ibid.,* XXXII, 392 (North Carolina; Cherokee Indian); Boggs, *ibid.,* XLVII, 298–99 (North Carolina; White); White and others, *The Frank C. Brown Collection of North Carolina Folklore,* I, 654–59; Federal Writers' Project of the Work Projects Administration, *South Carolina Folk Tales,* pp. 96–97 (Negro); Cox, *Southern Folklore Quarterly,* VII, 203–6 (West Virginia); Bandy, *Tennessee Folklore Society Bulletin,* IX, No. 2, 4–5 (Tennessee). In the Halpert collections there is a tape recording of an East Tennessee version. For a few British and Irish references (my notes on these are incomplete) see: Burne and Jackson, *Shropshire Folk-Lore,* pp. 157–58 (fragmentary, but see for notes on formulas); Kennedy, *Legendary Fictions of the Irish Celts,* pp. 148–50; Seymour, *Irish Witchcraft and Demonology,* pp. 233–35 (text is close to Kennedy, but abbreviated; see also for Scottish references). A Scottish version of the witch-imitator is referred to in *Choice Notes,* p. 80.

This tale of witch imitation is apparently a later development of an older story in which a man overhears the fairies' (or piskies') verbal formula for flying, repeats it, and so joins them in their travels, often to a wine cellar in some foreign land. Sometimes he returns safely with a cup from the cellar to prove he has been there; at other times he is caught and is to be hanged, but is rescued by a fairy (or pisky) woman, as in the witch-imitator form of the story.

A 1695 Scottish version was reported by the antiquarian John Aubrey, who died in 1697. See Aubrey, *Miscellanies upon Various Subjects* (4th edition; London, 1857), pp. 149–50. See also: *Choice Notes from Notes and Queries: Folk-Lore* (London, 1859), pp. 73–75 (Cornwall); Hunt, *Popular Romances of the West of England,* pp. 88–90, and reprinted in Hartland, *English Fairy and Other Folk Tales,* pp. 107–8 (Cornwall); Leather, *The Folk-Lore of Herefordshire,* pp. 176–77; *Choice Notes,* pp. 53–56 (Ireland). Only the formula and the flight (with "Trows") are given in Black and Thomas, *Examples of Printed Folk-Lore concerning the Orkney and Shetland Islands* (London, 1903), p. 21. (H.H.)

THERE'S BIGGER FOOLS THAN TILDY

Told by Mrs. Irene Carlisle, Springdale, Ark., April, 1951. She heard it from her grandmother about 1912. Recently Mrs. Carlisle made a tape recording of a similar item, as narrated by Mr. Jack Hughes, Buckner, Ark. Cf. *Arkansas Folklore,* II (May, 1952), 6, also the *Journal of American Folklore,* LXV (1952), 162. (V.R.)

This story combines a number of standard fool tales: Type 1450, "Clever Elsie"; Type 1384, "The Husband Hunts Three Persons as Stupid as His Wife"; Type 1284, "Jumping into the Breeches"; Type 1245, "Sunlight Carried in a Bag into the Windowless House"; Type 1326, "Moving the Church"; Type 1210, "The Cow is Taken to the Roof to Graze." These are often found together in much this combination; at other times they may be told independently. Since the bibliography for these tales is extremely long, I am not giving it in detail here. See: Clouston, *The Book of Noodles,* pp. 191–218; Gardner, *Folklore from the Schoharie Hills, New York,* pp. 163–72 (with good references); Parsons, *Antilles,* III, 309–10 (with references). There are unpublished versions from New Jersey, Kentucky, and Tennessee in the Halpert collections. (H.H.)

ON BREADTRAY MOUNTAIN

Told by Miss Rose O'Neill, Day, Mo., February, 1941. She got the tale from one of her neighbors, who was born and raised in the shadow of old Breadtray, a flat-topped elevation in Stone county, Mo., near the mouth of the James River.

Cf. the Breadtray Legend reported by Floyd M. Sullivan (Springfield, Mo., *Press,* Dec. 15, 1930); Sullivan credits it to Joseph H. Meredeth, an old-timer who spent his boyhood near Reeds Spring, Mo. Mary Elizabeth Mahnkey (Branson, Mo., *White River Leader,* Jan. 11, 1934) talked with a little girl in the 1890's who went up on Breadtray one night and heard "somethin' clankin' and rattlin' like plow blades." And then, writes Mrs. Mahnkey, "to my terror and amaze the child described the sound of a marching army, even the leathern screak of saddlery and holsters."

Tom Moore, familiar with the vicinity all his life, repeats the legend at great length (*Mysterious Tales and Legends of the Ozarks,* 1938, pp. 8–13). Judge Moore intimates that he heard the "sobs and moans and wailing screams" himself, for he says the tale "does not come from second-hand information, nor is it based upon hearsay."

Otto Ernest Rayburn (*Rayburn's Roadside Chats,* Beebe, Ark., Underhill Press, 1939, pp. 24–25) discusses the legend of Breadtray Mountain. In a later book (*Ozark Country,* 1941, pp. 197, 304–6) Rayburn tells four stories about Breadtray Mountain and says that the hillfolk avoid the place because they believe it is haunted.

I lived near Breadtray for several years, and mention the fireside tales about it in my *Ozark Superstitions* (1947, pp. 217–18). Once I spent most of the night on the mountain, but heard nothing out of the ordinary. (V.R.)

LITTLE THUMB AND THE GIANT

Told by Mr. Bob Wyrick, Eureka Springs, Ark., May, 1951. He heard it as a child near Green Forest, Ark., in the late 1890's. Cf. *Journal of American Folklore,* LXV (1952), 162–63. (V.R.)

This is a combination of Type 1115, "Attempted Murder with Hatchet," and Type 1088, "Eating Contest." The two incidents are often found together, as in the chapbook of Jack the Giant-Killer. English versions with these two incidents are given from chapbooks in Halliwell, *Popular Rhymes and Nursery Tales,* pp. 66–67; Jacobs, *English Fairy Tales,* pp. 102–3, No. 19; Hartland, *English Fairy and Other Folk Tales,* p. 7. The version in Leather, *The Folk-Lore of Herefordshire,* pp. 174–76, was collected from oral tradition, but was originally learned from a chapbook. Both types are found with many other incidents in Carrière, *Tales from the French Folk-Lore of Missouri,* pp. 270–78. Examples of Type 1115, combined with other giant-tricking incidents, are in Fauset, *Journal of American Folklore,* XL, 250 (Louisiana; Negro); MacManus, *The Well o' the World's End,* pp. 59–61 (Ireland). Type 1088 is found in Chase, *Jack Tales,* pp. 8–10 (North Carolina). For further references see my notes in Chase, *op. cit.,* p. 189. As I remark there, various adventures with giants (including this) are often combined with Type 1640, "The Brave Tailor." See also the study by Clouston, *Popular Tales and Fictions,* I, 133–54. (H.H.)

BANG AWAY, MY LULU!

Told by Mr. H. F. Walker, Joplin, Mo., July, 1923. He got it from members of a pioneer family near Sulphur Springs, Ark.

See a related tale in my *Ozark Superstitions* (1947, p. 296). Compare the "Beaten Jacket" story in *West Virginia Folklore,* a mimeographed bulletin issued by the West Virginia Folklore Society, Fairmont, W.Va., May, 1951, p. 2. (V.R.)

In a large number of witch stories an object is punished by whipping, e.g., a stalled cart or cream that will not turn to butter in a churn, and the witch who is causing the trouble feels the blows. Often a witch doctor or wise man prescribes or carries out the punishment. Webb, *New York Folklore Quarterly,* I, 9–10, tells of a sick child regular physicians could not cure. A witch doctor stripped the child, laid the clothes on the ground, and horsewhipped them. Next day the suspected witch was dead, her body covered with welts. (H.H.)

THE MARSHAL IN THE BARREL

Told by Mr. J. H. McGee, Joplin, Mo., July, 1934. He had it from a gambler who lived somewhere west of Fort Smith, Ark., in the 1890's.

This tale is rather widely known along the Arkansas-Oklahoma border. A similar story is printed in *Oklahoma, a Guide to the Sooner State* (1941, p. 116), only there it is a cowpuncher who is imprisoned and a buffalo which drags the barrel to the vicinity of a settlement. Cf. *Midwest Folklore,* II (Summer, 1952), 81–82. (V.R.)

This is a version of Type 1875, "The Boy on the Wolf's Tail." Boggs (*Journal of American Folklore,* XLVII, 273–74) reprints an early North Carolina version of this tale from *Fisher's River (North Carolina) Scenes and Characters,* by "Skitt" [H. E. Taliaferro], in which Indians put the man in a barrel and he catches hold of a bear's tail through the bunghole. It is train robbers and a bison's tail in the Colorado cowboy version given by Smith (*Publications of the Texas Folklore Society,* IX, 34–37). In a French-Canadian version translated by Greenough (*Canadian Folk-Life and Folk-Lore,* p. 48), the man, because he has no gun, creeps into a maple sugar hogshead to avoid a bear, then catches hold of the bear's tail and is taken for a ride. In an Alberta, Canada, version (*Alberta Folklore Quarterly,* I, 3), a man kills his horse, slits it open, and cleans it, then crawls inside to escape from freezing. He wakes to hear timber wolves gnawing at the frozen carcass. He catches the tails of two of the wolves, guides them back to his ranch, and there is freed from the frozen corpse. (H.H.)

ONE THING THEY CAN'T SELL

Told by Mr. Rufe Scott, Galena, Mo., April, 1942. He credits it to some courthouse loafers, who related it as an actual occurrence. (V.R.)

The spirit and theme of this story are somewhat parallel to the climax of the classic stanza about rationing in the days of the O.P.A. In the politer form of the limerick the "young lady of fashion" remarks to her lover, "Here's one thing that Henderson can't ration." (H.H.)

HEADING FOR TEXAS

Told by Mr. Otho Pratt, Verona, Mo., May, 1951. Mr. Pratt was raised in Stone county, Mo., and heard this tale somewhere on Horse Creek in the early 1900's. (V.R.)

An unpublished New Jersey variant of this tale is in the Halpert collections. (H.H.)

HOW TOODIE FIXED OLD GRUNT

Told by Mr. R. H. Robertson, Joplin, Mo., January, 1938. He got it from a girl who heard many such tales in Benton county, Ark., about 1895. Cf. *Midwest Folklore*, II (Summer, 1952), 82–83. (V.R).

This appears to be a much reduced version of the Bluebeard story, Type 312, "The Giant-killer and His Dog (Bluebeard)," with a lover replacing the brother as the rescuer. The girl's trick of blinding her murderous husband is reminiscent of Daniel Boone's trick for escaping from his Indian captors. (H.H.)

THE INFIDEL'S GRAVE

Told by Mr. Ern Long, Joplin, Mo., August, 1931. He said it was common, in several versions, all over southern Missouri. Rayburn (*Ozark Guide*, Spring, 1950, p. 29) prints a related tale from Hot Springs, Ark. See also Earl A. Collins (*Legends and Lore of Missouri*, 1951, pp. 57–59). Cf. *Midwest Folklore*, II (Summer, 1952), 83–84. (V.R.)

This well-known tale, a form of Motif N 384, "Death from fright," is usually vouched for as an actual occurrence. A girl (or boy), to show her bravery, is to jab a fork (or knife, stick, etc.) into a grave, or drive a nail into a coffin; she accidentally pins her dress, or coat, to the ground or coffin and dies of fear. Smith, *Hoosier Folklore*, VI, 107, gives several American and European references. For American versions see Fauset, *Journal of American*

Folklore, XLI, 548 (Philadelphia; Negro, learned in North Carolina); Boggs, *ibid.*, XLVII, 295–96 (North Carolina; two variants); White and others, *The Frank C. Brown Collection of North Carolina Folklore*, I, 686; Federal Writers' Project of the Work Projects Administration, *South Carolina Folk Tales*, pp. 103–4 (Negro); Halpert, *Hoosier Folklore Bulletin*, I, 58–59 (Indiana); Neely and Spargo, *Tales and Songs of Southern Illinois*, pp. 64–67 (four variants); Dorson, *Hoosier Folklore*, VI, 5 (Wisconsin; learned in Hanover, Germany); *ibid.*, 5, note 1 (Professor Dorson refers to at least four variants which he heard in Michigan); Baylor, *ibid.*, 144 (New Mexico; Spanish; told as religious tale); Klein, *New Mexico Folklore Record*, VI, 27 (New Mexico; from Hungary). Jansen (*Hoosier Folklore Bulletin*, II, 8) gives a curious Pennsylvania version told in Indiana, in which a grave robber pins his own long coattails to the ground with his shovel, and, of course, dies.

Another version of this tale ends with the man who is proving his courage going mad rather than dying. See: Saxon, Dreyer, and Tallant, *Gumbo Ya-Ya*, pp. 276–77 (Louisiana); Law, *Folk-Lore*, XI, 346 (Wiltshire, England); *ibid.*, 346, note 2 (from south of Ireland). (H.H.)

JACK AND THE SACK

Told by Mrs. Ethel Barnes, Hot Springs, Ark., April, 1938. She had it from relatives who lived in Garland county, Ark., in the 1880's. Cf. *Journal of American Folklore*, LXV (1952), 159–60.

See *Ozark Guide* (Winter, 1946, p. 219) for a related story about a man who was tied and blindfolded on a scaffold, waiting to be hanged. He somehow talked a spectator into releasing him and taking his place. The rope breaks, however, so as to provide the story with a relatively happy ending. (V.R.)

This plot is found as incident VI in Type 1542, "The Clever Boy," or incident V in Type 1535, "The Rich and the Poor Peasant." For other versions see my notes in this book to "The Magic Cowhide," a text of Type 1535 which lacks this incident. For other versions in which the incident appears as an independent story or in combination with others, see: Brendle and Troxell, *Pennsylvania*

189

German Folk Tales, pp. 172–73; Aiken, *Publications of the Texas Folklore Society,* XII, 34–35, 54–55 (Mexican; Spanish; some of Mr. Aiken's stories were collected on the Texas side of the border). A variant of the story in Mr. Randolph's note, of the man on the gallows who gets someone to take his place, appears in Boggs, *Journal of American Folklore,* XLVII, 309 (North Carolina). (H.H.)

THE WOMAN IN THE BED

Told by Mr. Lon Jordan, Farmington, Ark., October, 1941. He said it was "an old ghost story" that he heard in Fayetteville, Ark., about 1905. Cf. *Journal of American Folklore,* LXV (1952), 160. (V.R.)

A TALL FELLOW'S TURKEY

Told by Mr. Charles S. Hiatt, Cassville, Mo., April, 1933. He heard it in the early 1900's, not far from Cassville. "It might be a true story, for all I know," said he. "And then again, it might not." (V.R.)

This is one version of the story of "The Master Thief": 1525 D, "The Man Betrays the Thieves." Two North Carolina versions are in Chase, *Jack Tales,* pp. 114–26 (a composite), and pp. 195–97 (a text written down by an informant). Both texts combine, though in different ways, the A and D forms of Type 1525. My notes in Chase, *op. cit.,* p. 195, cover both forms, but primarily the A one. For supplementary references see the following. Parsons, *Antilles,* III, 215–17, has abstracts of both the A and D forms as well as excellent comparative notes. The two forms are combined in the text in Carrière, *Tales from the French Folk-Lore of Missouri,* pp. 285–89. For Type 1525 A add: Anderson, *Southern Workman,* XXVIII, 232–33 (Southern Negro); Parsons, *Folk-Lore of the Sea Islands, South Carolina,* pp. 112–13 (Negro); Gomme, *Folk-Lore,* XX, 76 (Durham, England); MacManus, *In Chimney Corners,* pp. 207–23 (Ireland). There is an old English jestbook version in *Merie Tales of Skelton,* reprinted in *Shakespeare Jest-Books* (ed. by W. C. Hazlitt), II, 22–23.

190

Type 1525 D has been studied by Clouston, *Popular Tales and Fictions,* II, 43–52. He gives (pp. 43–44) a version from an English magazine. Add: Cutting, *New York Folklore Quarterly,* VII, 62 (New York); Boggs, *Journal of American Folklore,* XLVII, 308 (North Carolina); MacManus, *op. cit.,* pp. 149–56 (Ireland; this also has Incident II of the A form). For an eighteenth-century Scottish chapbook version, see "The Comical Tricks of Lothian Tom," pp. 15–18, in John Cheap, *The Chapman's Library.* (H.H.)

SOME OTHER SMALL GUT

Told by Mr. Otho Pratt, Verona, Mo., May, 1951. He heard this anecdote in Stone county, Mo., about 1910. (V.R.)

This is distantly related to Type 1696, "What Should I Have Said? (Done?)," with, however, a fortunate outcome for the fool. For some references to Type 1696, see my notes in Chase, *Jack Tales,* pp. 192–93. There are several English tales of fools who search for wives, usually without success, but none that I know are very close to this Ozark tale. (H.H.)

BIG KNIVES IN ARKANSAS

Told by Mr. C. P. Mahnkey, Mincy, Mo., November, 1939. Mr. Mahnkey had it from his neighbors in Taney county, Mo., not far from the Missouri-Arkansas border.

I published a shorter version of this tale in *Funny Stories from Arkansas* (1943, p. 23). A slightly different text, written by the wife of my informant, appeared in *Ozark Guide* (Autumn, 1945, p. 122). Cf. *Midwest Folklore,* II (Summer, 1952), 84–85. (V.R.)

LOCUSTS GOT THE CORN

Told by Miss Marion Neville, Chesterton, Ind., November, 1950. This is one of the "teaser stories" that her father used to tell the children at Springfield, Mo., in the early 1900's. Judge Neville had it from *his* father, born in Kentucky in 1816. "I don't even know if locusts eat corn," says Miss Neville, "but they do in this story."

A familiar type of bedtime story, an answer to boys and girls who set up a clamor for entertainment. Such tales are drawled out in a deliberately sedative, hypnotic monotone; no attention is paid to interruptions or comments. If the storyteller sticks to his last, the child soon falls asleep. (V.R.)

This is a well-known form of Type 2300, "Endless Tales." Carl Sandburg gives a version in *The People, Yes* (New York, 1936), pp. 205–6. In the references that follow I have indicated any variation from the locusts and grains-of-corn pattern. See: Brendle and Troxell, *Pennsylvania German Folk Tales,* p. 34 (cockroach and wheat; variant has weevil); Halpert, *Southern Folklore Quarterly,* VIII, 109–10 (Mississippi); Halpert, *Hoosier Folklore Bulletin,* I, 33 (Indiana); *ibid.,* 33–34 (Indiana; ants); Federal Writers' Project of the Work Projects Administration, *Idaho Lore,* pp. 148–50 (Idaho Indians; ant and corn); Espinosa, *Journal of American Folklore,* XLIX, 101–3 (Pueblo Indians; ants and grains of wheat); Lanctôt, *ibid.,* XLIV, 262 (Canadian-French; locusts and oats); Lambert, *ibid.,* LIII, 157 (Canadian-French; locusts and oats); Addy, *Household Tales,* p. 15 (Nottinghamshire, England); *Handbook of Irish Folklore,* p. 588 (bird; ant). Compare: Halpert, *Hoosier Folklore Bulletin,* I, 69 (Kentucky; crows). This last is not an endless tale but an apologue in which all the corn is finally taken, leaving the miser only cobs. (H.H.)

THE TIME THE RED MEN RODE

Told by Mr. H. F. Walker, Joplin, Mo., July, 1923. He had it from old-timers at Sulphur Springs, Ark., but believes the tale originated in "some little shikepoke town" along the Arkansas-Oklahoma border.

It seems that this piece of business was known in many parts of the Middle West. My mother witnessed a similar incident in Girard, Kan., about 1880, and her father was one of the "Indians." See Stanley Vestal (*Queen of the Cow Towns,* 1952, pp. 82–85) for an account of the "Indian Act" at Dodge City, Kan., in 1877. (V.R.)

192

JOB WAS PRETTY STINGY

Told by Mr. J. H. McGee, Joplin, Mo., July, 1934. He got it from some children in Christian county, Mo., about 1902. (V.R.)

In two other versions of this bunghole trick story, one from North Carolina published by Boggs (*Journal of American Folklore,* XLVII, 308), the other from Nova Scotia given by Creighton (*Folklore of Lunenberg County, Nova Scotia,* p. 132), the dupe brings the situation on himself. In neither of these does the wife take advantage of the man's being occupied. In the thirteenth tale of the famous chapbook of the Mad Men of Gotham (reprinted in Stapleton, *All About the Merry Tales of Gotham* [Nottingham, 1900], p. 24, and by many other editors), the husband bets his wife that she can't make him a cuckold. She pulls the bunghole trick on him. After completing her part of the bet with a tailor, she brings a spigot to her husband to release him and to tell him he has lost his wager. A version of the story (in its milder form) is in a local ballad from New York given by Wheeler (*New York Folklore Quarterly,* X, 116–17). For similar tales also compare the *Handbook of Irish Folklore,* p. 586.

It would be incorrect to classify any of these tales as Type 1731, "The Youth and the Pretty Shoes," even though the latter has such motifs as seduced women and a bunghole trick. In the Type form (see Parsons, *Folk-Tales of Andros Island, Bahamas,* p. 150), *first* all of the women of the house are seduced in easy succession, and *then* the male head of the household is tricked. This is quite different from the structure of the Ozark and Gotham tales in which the wife's behavior is contingent upon the husband's being kept out of circulation by a trick. (H.H.)

A PRETTY GIRL IN THE ROAD

Told by Mr. Tom Shiras, Mountain Home, Ark., September 1941. He said it was a "foolish ghost story" popular at Mountain Home about 1930. Cf. *Journal of American Folklore,* LXV (1952), 163–64, reprinted in *Ozark Guide,* Autumn, 1952, pp. 23–24. See also the *Arkansas Gazette* (July 29, 1953) for an account of a similar hitchhiking ghost on the highway between Little Rock and Pine Bluff, Ark. (V.R.)

This is a version of "The Vanishing Hitchhiker," which in its various forms is probably the ghost story in most vigorous circulation today in America. I have not attempted to collect and classify the many references appearing in the folklore journals and in more popular print. A large number of variants were assembled and studied by Richard K. Beardsley and Rosalie Hankey (*California Folklore Quarterly,* I, 303–35, II, 13–26) and by Louis C. Jones (*ibid.,* III, 284–92). Mr. Beardsley and Miss Hankey believe this is a strictly modern story. Dr. Jones, who also offers European versions, contends it has merely been adapted to modern automobile transportation from early stories belonging to the age of transportation by horse. The Halpert collections have a large number of Kentucky ghost stories in which a ghost jumps on the horse in back of its rider, or takes a ride as passenger in a buggy. These older stories apparently support Dr. Jones's contention. (H.H.)

GROUNDHOG CHARLEY

Told by Mr. Frank Payne, Galena, Mo., November, 1932. He heard the tale in Taney county, Mo., about 1910. Mr. Frank Pickett, Eureka Springs, Ark., tells a different version: a local man shaved off his handlebar mustache and thus learned of his wife's readiness to accept smooth-shaven strangers. Cf. *Midwest Folklore,* II (Summer, 1952), 85–86. (V.R.)

A North Carolina version given by Boggs (*Journal of American Folklore,* XLVII, 306–7) differs chiefly in that the farmer, in town on a Saturday, is not made drunk, but merely persuaded to get his whiskers shaved and his hair clipped short. Hayes (*New York Folklore Quarterly,* IX, 42) tells of a New York character who cut off his tremendous beard because he "lost too many vittles in it." He said that the morning after he cut it off his wife didn't know him and thought she had been sleeping with a stranger. He had to regrow his whiskers " 'fore she was satisfied her morals was what they should be." (H.H.)

194

Told by Mrs. Marie Wilbur, Pineville, Mo., July, 1930. She had it from an old woman in McDonald county, Mo. Cf. *Midwest Folklore*, II (Summer, 1952), 86–87. (V.R.)

This tale I classify as a version of Type 559, "Dungbeetle." A North Carolina text was published by Boggs (*Journal of American Folklore*, XLVII, 297), and there are unpublished versions from New York and New Jersey in the Halpert collections. Professor E. W. Baughman refers me to Dempster, *Folk-Lore Journal*, VI, 183–84, for a version of this type from Sutherland. Professor Baughman, however, classifies the Boggs version under Type 571, "Making the Princess Laugh: 'All Stick Together.'" There is a North Carolina text of Type 571 in Chase (*Jack Tales*, pp. 83–88) for which I supplied notes on p. 192. To my references add: Brendle and Troxell, *Pennsylvania German Folk Tales*, pp. 30–31; Mac-Manus, *Donegal Fairy Stories*, pp. 217–30 (Ireland). (H.H.)

BOOTS ON THE WIRE

Told by Mr. Ed Wall, Pineville, Mo., August, 1924. He heard it near Noel, Mo., in the early 1900's.

This story must be pretty recent, for the old-timers say that telegraph wires were unknown in the Ozarks until the 1860's. Stith Thompson (*The Folktale*, 1946, p. 192) says that the tale has been reported from Russia and "is presumably current in Spain." It is common in the Ozarks today, and I think in other parts of the South. See a variant in Thomas W. Jackson (*Through Missouri on a Mule* (1946, p. 57); the first edition of this book appeared in 1904. Cf. *Southern Folklore Quarterly*, XVI (1952), 166–67. (V.R.)

Motif J 1935.1, "Boots sent by telegraph." Wilson (*Folk-Lore*, XLIX, 188) mentions that the story appears in the second part of a nineteenth-century collection of dialect stories from Westmorland, England. (H.H.)

THE MAGIC HORN

Told by Dr. O. St. John, Pineville, Mo., July, 1921. He got it from some of the old settlers on Big Sugar Creek, near Cyclone, Mo. (V.R.)

The trickster theme of selling the life-restoring object, though occasionally found independently, is usually found as an incident in Type 1542, "The Clever Boy" (Incident IV), and also in Type 1535, "The Rich and the Poor Peasant" (Incident IVb). It occurs, for example, in Boggs, *Journal of American Folklore,* XLVII, 308–9 (North Carolina); Fauset, *ibid.,* 253 (Louisiana; Negro); Aiken, *Publications of the Texas Folklore Society,* XII, 32–33 (Mexican; Spanish); Campbell, *Popular Tales of the West Highlands,* II, 232–36 (Highland Scotland; three variants). See Parsons, *Antilles,* III, 213–14, for eight abstracts and further references. The references to "The Magic Cowhide" in this book should also be checked for other examples of this incident. (H.H.)

THERE WAS AN OLD WOMAN

Told by Mr. Lon Jordan, Farmington, Ark., October, 1941. It was a common story around Fayetteville, Ark., he says, some time before 1910. (V.R.)

THE TOADFROG

Told by Miss Mary C. Parler, Fayetteville, Ark., May, 1951. She had it from a student at the University of Arkansas.

This seems to be a retelling of Grimm's "Der Froschkönig," with a modern wisecrack ending. Compare a similar tale in Christina Stead's novel *Letty Fox* (1946, p. 296). Joey Adams (*From Gags to Riches,* 1949, pp. 89–90) tells the same story with a turtle instead of a frog. See also W. H. Elzey (*Things about Things,* n.d., pp. 77–78) and J. M. Elgart (*Over Sixteen* (1951, p. 34). Cf. *Journal of American Folklore* LXV (1952), 164. (V.R.)

This is Type 440, "The Frog King or Iron Henry," with (as Mr. Randolph remarks) a modern wisecrack ending. In a recent joke book (*Funny Side Up* [1952], p. 136) we have the princess and the golden ball and the frog who goes to sleep in her golden bed. Next morning she finds a beautiful prince next to her. "And to this day her mother won't believe the story of the frog." A frog suitor who turns into a prince is in Carter (*Journal of American Folklore*, XXXVIII, 272, "The Louse Skin"), but the story is a version of Type 425 B. Versions of the standard form of the tale are not common in the American and British tradition. It is reported from Scotland by Chambers (*Popular Rhymes of Scotland*, pp. 87–89) and Campbell (*Popular Tales of the West Highlands*, II, 130–35). The version by Jacobs (*English Fairy Tales*, pp. 215–19, No. 41) is a composite text based on Leyden's edition of *The Complaynt of Scotland* and Halliwell. In the version by Halliwell (*Popular Rhymes and Nursery Tales*, pp. 43–47) only the rhymes are from oral tradition in the north of England; the "framework" is by Halliwell. A good English *cante fable* text from Holderness in Yorkshire appears unexpectedly in the "Notes" in W. H. Jones and L. L. Kropf, *The Folk-Tales of the Magyars* (London, 1889), pp. 404–5, n. (The text includes elements from Type 403, "The Black and the White Bride.") The tale is also known in Ireland (*Handbook of Irish Folklore*, p. 563), and by Negroes in Martinique and Dominica (Parsons, *Antilles*, III, 233–34). (H.H.)

OLD BLACK-OAK KNOWS BEST

Told by Mr. Frank Payne, Galena, Mo., November, 1932. He heard it in Stone county, Mo., about 1904. "Folks used to spin lots of tales like that when I was young," said he. I published this text in the *Southern Folklore Quarterly*, XVI (1952), 165–66. (V.R.)

This is a form of Type 1476, "The Prayer for a Husband." Various forms of this widespread tale are listed under Motif K 1971. In a version given by Gardner (*Folklore from the Schoharie Hills, New York*, pp. 175–77), the poor boy hides himself in the church loft and on three separate occasions advises the girl who has been praying for a husband that he should be chosen. Gardner points out the relationship between her New York text and a tale from Derbyshire, England, given by Addy (*Household Tales*, p. 30) which in turn resembles one in the Grimm collection. In these a girl is praying for her husband. When answered negatively by a man who overhears her prayers, she thinks the speaker is the child, Mary (or the infant Jesus), and orders it to be silent and let its mother speak. In an undated Glasgow chapbook (*Grinning Made Easy*, p. 9, reprinted in the Comic and Humorous volume of John Cheap, *The Chapman's Library*) a widow, who had sworn to remain single, prays to the image of the Virgin for permission to remarry. A concealed wag answers, "No." The widow immediately replies, "Hold your tongue, you bastard; I am speaking to your mother." The anti-Catholic bias of these last three stories (English, German, and Scottish) is obvious. The religious element has dropped out of the Ozark story. A Yorkshire version given by Mrs. Gutch (*Examples of Printed Folk-Lore concerning the North Riding of Yorkshire, York and the Ainsty* [London, 1901; *Publications of the Folk-Lore Society,* Vol. XLV], p. 220) has the retort as in Addy, but with an added touch. The woman prays for any husband except a tailor, but finally replies (to the remarks of the supposed little Jesus) that she'll take a tailor rather than nothing. (H.H.)

THE GOOD GIRL AND THE ORNERY GIRL

Told by Miss Callista O'Neill, Day, Mo., September, 1941. She had it from some old settlers who lived on Bear Creek, Taney county, Mo., in the early 1900's.

This is pretty much like Grimm's "Frau Holle." The cow is not mentioned in Grimm, but it does appear in the related "Lazy Maria" tale which Gardner (*Folklore from the Schoharie Hills, New York,* 1937, pp. 123–26) found in New York. (V.R.)

This is an abbreviated version of Type 480, "The Spinning Woman by the Spring," allied with Section II of Type 403, "The Black and the White Bride." Dr. Warren Roberts studied Type 480 for his doctoral dissertation at Indiana University (1953). He has been kind enough to verify some references for me and to furnish me with several I had overlooked. In turn, I was able to supply some texts that he did not have.

This Ozark text, like Gardner's New York text, mentioned above by Mr. Randolph, is close to the German forms of the tale. Dr. Roberts writes that the version in Patrick Kennedy, *The Fireside Stories of Ireland* (Dublin, 1870), pp. 33–37 (which I have not seen), is very similar to the Grimms' form. Parson, *Antilles,* III, 225–29, gives exhaustive, world-wide references, mainly to Type 403, under the title "The Good Child and the Bad." The Louisiana French text given by Fortier (*Louisiana Folk-Tales,* pp. 117–19) was reprinted by Botkin (*A Treasury of American Folklore,* pp. 676–78).

American and British versions of Type 480 seem to fall into two groups. In the first form, "the three heads of the well," the good girl washes and wipes gently three heads (skeletons, fish, etc.) that bob up in a well—and is rewarded. The bad girl is unkind and is punished. For American versions see: L. Roberts, *Mountain Life & Work,* XXVII, No. 1 (Winter, 1951), 25–28 (Kentucky mountains); Dobie, *Publications of the Texas Folklore Society,* VI, 42–45 (Texas); Lowrimore, *California Folklore Quarterly,* IV, 155 (fragmentary; California; learned in Arkansas). This form of the tale has a long literary history in England. Halliwell and Jacobs pointed out it was found in George Peele's *The Old Wives' Tale,* and Mrs. Bertha Dobie refers to a study which I have not seen: "Peele's Use of Folk-Lore in *The Old Wives' Tale,* by Sarah Clapp, in *Studies in English,* University of Texas, No. 6, pp. 146–56. The story has also circulated in chapbooks; see Cunningham, *Amusing Prose Chapbooks,* pp. 193–97. An abridged chapbook version is given in Halliwell (*Popular Rhymes and Nursery Tales,* pp. 39–43), from which it was reprinted, somewhat changed, in Jacobs (*English Fairy Tales,* pp. 222–27, No. 43). A slightly different chapbook apparently was the source for the version in Hartland (*English Fairy and Other Folk Tales,* pp. 20–24). British and Irish texts from oral tradition are in: Gomme, *Folk-Lore,* VII, 411–14 (Hertford); Chambers, *Popular Rhymes of Scotland,* pp. 105–7; Flower, *The Western Island,* pp. 64–70 (Great Blasket Island, Ireland). Dr. Warren Roberts also refers me to other Irish texts in *Béaloideas.*

The second, or "long leather bag," form of this *cante fable* seems rather more popular than the first form in the British-

199

American oral tradition. In it the good girl (or boy), after being kind to a cow, tree, etc., looks up the chimney of a witch's house and gets a long leather bag full of gold. She flees with it, and is pursued by the witch, but the animals, tree, etc., conceal her. The bad girl is unkind and is revealed and punished. For American versions see: Conant, *Journal of American Folklore*, VIII, 143–44 (Massachusetts); Carter, *ibid.*, XXXVIII, 368–70 (North Carolina); Chase, *Grandfather Tales*, pp. 18–27 (North Carolina and Virginia: composite text); L. Roberts, *Mountain Life & Work*, XXVIII, No. 4 (Autumn, 1952), 24–28 (Kentucky mountains). An unpublished text from West Kentucky is in the Halpert collections. For British and Irish versions see: Jacobs, *More English Fairy Tales*, pp. 94–98, No. 64 (from Deptford; Jacobs also notes, p. 230, that he dimly recalls hearing it in Australia); Gerish, *Folk-Lore*, VII, 414–15 (Norfolk?); Addy, *Household Tales*, pp. 11–12 (Nottinghamshire); *ibid.*, pp. 18–22 (Derbyshire); Henderson, *Notes on the Folklore of the Northern Counties of England and the Borders* (1879 ed.), pp. 349–50 (Northumberland); Grice, *Folk Tales of the North Country*, pp. 108–10 (apparently taken from Henderson with slight changes); *Miscellanea of the Rymour Club*, Edinburgh, II, 200–201 (lowland Scotland); MacManus, *Donegal Fairy Stories*, pp. 233–56 (Ireland); *Handbook of Irish Folklore*, p. 619, No. 34. (H.H.)

MISTER FOX

Told by Mrs. Mary Burke, Springfield, Mo., May, 1932. She credited it to relatives who lived in Christian county, Mo., in the 1880's and 1890's.

Isabel Spradley and I published a similar riddle (*Journal of American Folklore*, XLVII [1934], 84) with the note: "This rhyme is concerned with an old story about a woman who saw her lover digging a grave to bury her in." Two Ozark versions of the riddle appear in a paper by Archer Taylor and me (*Southern Folklore Quarterly*, VIII [1944], 8). Cf. *Midwest Folklore*, II (Summer, 1952), 87–89. (V.R.)

This is one of the three related ways in which the story best classified as Type 955, "The Robber Bridegroom," is told in the Anglo-American tradition. Since the three versions are related in complicated fashion, I give here references to all three forms. Only the first of these versions clearly fits the "type" story; but several scholars have demonstrated that versions two and three are closely linked to the pattern.

The type form of the story, often called "Mr. Fox," is usually marked by the formula, "Be bold, be bold, but not too bold." (Occasionally there is also a second formula.) The girl visits her lover's house in his absence and finds he is a robber and murderer. Later at a party she reveals the facts by telling the story as if it were a dream. See: Gardner, *Folklore from the Schoharie Hills, New York*, pp. 146–55, for a New York text and discussion; Carter, *Journal of American Folklore*, XXXVIII, 360–61 (North Carolina). A Texas version in MS is mentioned in Dobie, *Publications of the Texas Folklore Society*, VI, 55. There are English versions in *Choice Notes from Notes and Queries: Folk-Lore* (London, 1859), pp. 138–40 (Kent); Halliwell, *Popular Rhymes and Nursery Tales*, pp. 47–48; Hartland, *English Fairy and Other Folk Tales*, pp. 25–27; Jacobs, *English Fairy Tales*, pp. 148–51, No. 26. The last three texts are reprints of the version which Blakeway contributed to Malone's variorum *Shakspeare* (1821) to elucidate a speech in *Much Ado About Nothing*. The "be bold" formula, probably referring to this story, is also found in Spenser's *Faerie Queene*, Book III, Canto 11, stanza 54. An outline of the story, possibly from oral tradition, is given with interesting comment in Violet Alford, *Introduction to English Folklore* (London, 1952), pp. 143–45.

Mr. Randolph's text belongs to the second or tale-with-rhyme version of the story. A girl comes early to a rendezvous with her lover, climbs a tree, and observes him digging her grave. Later she reveals her knowledge in a rhyme which usually mentions a hole "the fox" did make. For American and English versions see: Carter, *op. cit.*, p. 372 (Tennessee); Halliwell, *op. cit.*, pp. 49–50 (Oxfordshire); Addy, *Household Tales, with Other Traditional Remains* (London and Sheffield, 1895), pp. 10–11 (Derbyshire).

201

Occasionally the rhyme section is sung, thus making the story a true *cante fable,* as in Kidson, *Journal of the Folk-Song Society,* II, 297–98 (Yorkshire; see pp. 298–99, for a Sussex text given by A. G. Gilchrist). Kidson notes that there are very full references to the story in *Notes and Queries,* (7th series, Vol. iii, 1887, pp. 149, 229, 410). I have not seen these recently, but many of the verses from them are reprinted in Northall, *English Folk-Rhymes* (London, 1892), pp. 533–35. To a query in *Word-Lore* I (1926), 33, which gave a text of a sung fragment of the verse without the tale, Miss A. G. Gilchrist replied (*Word-Lore,* I, 71–72), with a discussion of the relation between the tale and the tale-with-rhyme forms of the story. Her discussion recapitulates much of the information in the Kidson article noted above.

Closely related to the second version (the *cante fable* form of this story) is the "neck riddle" form. In this third version the tale becomes the answer to, or explanation of, a riddle. For discussion of this type and references see: Halpert, *Southern Folklore Quarterly,* V, 198–99, and note 23; Norton, *Folk-Lore,* LIII, 27–57; White and others, *The Frank C. Brown Collection of North Carolina Folklore,* I, 308–9, and note. (H.H.)

THE BULL WAS FOUND GUILTY

Told by Mr. Price Paine, Noel, Mo., October, 1923. He heard it near Noel in the late 1890's.

Stories of animal trials are not uncommon. John R. Musick (*Stories of Missouri,* 1897, pp. 164–65) tells a related tale in which a dog was tried for stealing meat. H. Allen Smith (*The Compleat Practical Joker,* 1953, pp. 92–93) says that the people in Raymond, Miss., tried a bedbug for biting Judge Gohlson; the trial lasted four hours, and the bedbug was acquitted.

The "bull trial" story is told as the truth today, but the published accounts are not very well documented. Otto Ernest Rayburn (*Arcadian Magazine,* November, 1931, p. 15) credits the tale to Jim Winn of Winslow, Ark., who says the trial was held in Washington county, Ark., and "is on record in the courthouse at Fayetteville." Charles Morrow Wilson (*Backwoods America,*

1934, pp. 150–51) places it "in the justice court of Squire Nottingham, who held sway in Cove Creek township," Washington county, Ark. In his book *Ozark Country* (1941, pp. 32–33), Rayburn reprints the yarn, saying that the bull was tried "in the Boston Mountains of Arkansas" in the 1880's. "It is not a tall tale from the windy hilltops," he writes, "but can be verified by persons still living." (V.R.)

J. F. Campbell (*Popular Tales of the West Highlands,* II, 381) refers to a Gaelic story in which "some women, as judges, doomed a horse to be hanged." He first was stolen; but the thief, as a first offender, got off. Then the horse, evidently preferring the thief as master, left his rightful owner and went to the thief's house again, but this time by himself. The horse was condemned for stealing himself. Wright (*Rustic Speech and Folk-Lore* [London, 1913], p. 182) has a proverbial comparison in North Lincolnshire dialect which implies a story related to the Gaelic one. In English "translation" it runs: "As foolish as the men of Belton, who hanged a sheep for stealing a man." (H.H.)

WHEN LIZZIE PICKED THE GREENS

Told by Mrs. Marie Wilbur, Pineville, Mo., March, 1931. She had it from one of her neighbors on Big Sugar Creek, in McDonald county, Mo. (V.R.)

THE BOY AND THE TURKEYS

Told by Mr. Rex Thomas, Lamar, Mo., November, 1934. He credits it to Mr. Arthur Aull, editor of the Lamar *Democrat.*

The tale was published by Bryan and Rose (*Pioneer Families of Missouri,* 1876, p. 508) as heard in Callaway county, Mo. I used a variant from Little Rock, Ark., in a pamphlet *Funny Stories from Arkansas* (1943, p. 15). See also a reference in my *We Always Lie to Strangers* (1947, pp. 122–23). (V.R.)

This is a version of Type 1881, "The Man Carried Through the Air by Geese." In most of the American versions listed below the man is catching geese, occasionally ducks, and only rarely turkeys. In many of the texts we have the theme combined with

Type 1900, "How the Man Came out of a Tree Stump." There is a fine literary handling of a North Carolina version of the story by William Gilmore Simms, "How Sharp Snaffles Got His Capital and His Wife," *Harper's New Monthly Magazine*, XLI (October, 1870), 667–87, and abstracted in Dorson, *California Folklore Quarterly*, IV, 211. For an orally collected version of Simms's story, recorded in South Carolina, see Botkin, *A Treasury of Southern Folklore*, p. 464. For other versions see: Selby, *100 Goofy Lies*, p. 26; Cutting, *Lore of an Adirondack County*, p. 28 (New York); Boggs, *Journal of American Folklore*, XLVII, 315 (North Carolina); Chase, *Grandfather Tales*, pp. 180–81 and 184 (North Carolina; ducks); Chase, *Jack Tales*, pp. 151–52 and 156 (North Carolina; turkeys); A. M. Trout, "Greetings," *Louisville Courier-Journal*, February 11, 1953 (Butler County, Kentucky); Butler, *Hoosier Folklore*, VII, 36–37 (Indiana; turkeys); Jagendorf, *Sand in the Bag*, p. 81 (Indiana; turkeys); Greenough, *Canadian Folk-Life and Folk-Lore*, pp. 49–50 (Quebec, Canada; French; ducks); Gard, *Johnny Chinook*, pp. 300–302 (Alberta, Canada).

There are also some peculiar variations to this theme which are worth noting. In one form a man finds geese trapped in the ice and is carried off by them when the ice cake breaks loose. See Thomas, *Tall Stories*, pp. 185–87 (New York); *ibid.*, p. 187 (New Brunswick, Canada); House, *Tall Talk from Texas*, p. 12 (Texas). In a Texas story a cowboy catches buzzards and has them haul him out of a sink hole. See Boatright, *Tall Tales from Texas*, pp. 59–64; House, *op. cit.*, pp. 8–9. In another tale an eel is used as bait and passes in succession through a series of geese, which then fly off with the man. See Dorson, *Jonathan Draws the Long Bow*, p. 229, note 20 (from an 1833 comic almanac). Compare Jansen, *Hoosier Folklore Bulletin*, II, 6–7 (Indiana). In the latter the bait is a piece of fat on a line, and it is ducks that are caught. For a 1751 discussion of this method of trapping ducks, see Emery, *Hoosier Folklore Bulletin*, III, 23. (H.H.)

ARITHMETIC ON BEAR CREEK

Told by Miss Callista O'Neill, Day, Mo., September, 1941. She had it from her neighbors on Bear Creek, Taney county, Mo., in the early 1900's. See a similar tale in *Anecdota Americana* (1934, p. 123). (V.R.)

GRIND THE COFFEE

Told by Mrs. Mary Burke, Springfield, Mo., May, 1932. It was related in Christian county, Mo., she says, about 1910.

Similar to the "noodle story" about the man who sawed off the limb upon which he sat, this yarn is widely known, usually told as the experience of some local character. Bryan and Rose (*Pioneer Families of Missouri*, 1876, p. 389) print a similar tale about Thomas Benton Young, who lived in Audrain county, Mo., in the 1830's. "The fall jolted him so severely," we are told, "that he never entirely recovered from it, and did not make as great a man as his distinguished namesake." Cf. *Southern Folklore Quarterly*, XVI (1952), 170–71. (V.R.)

This yarn, as Mr. Randolph points out, resembles an internationally-known tale: Type 1240 (Motif J 2133.4), "Man Sitting on Branch of Tree Cuts It Off." Although British and American versions of the standard form of the tale have been reported, I know of no other examples of Mr. Randolph's version. (H.H.)

THE MAGIC COWHIDE

Told by Mr. Lon Jordan, Farmington, Ark., November, 1941. He heard it near Fayetteville, Ark., in 1903. Cf. *Journal of American Folklore*, LXV (1952), 165–66. (V.R.)

This is a version of Type 1535, "The Rich and the Poor Peasant." It lacks two incidents frequently found in full versions of the type: IVb, Fatal Imitation, and V, Fatal Deception. Both of these appear as independent stories in this book; see "The Magic Horn" for the first, and "Jack and the Sack" for the second. My notes to these stories supplement those given below.

Chase (*Jack Tales*, pp. 161–71) gives a North Carolina text for which I furnished many references on pp. 199–200. The following notes can be added. The North Carolina text in Botkin (*A Treasury of Southern Folklore*, pp. 519–25) is of particular interest, since it was transcribed from a recording made by Mrs. Maude Long, daughter of Mrs. Jane Gentry. It may be compared with Mrs. Gentry's text, which was published in 1925 by Carter (*Journal of American Folklore*, XXXVIII, 343–46). See also: Carrière, *Tales from the French Folk-Lore of Missouri*, pp. 290–96; Lowrimore, *California Folklore Quarterly*, IV, 156–57 (California; learned in Arkansas); Aiken, *Publications of the Texas Folklore Society*, XII, 36–41 (Mexican; Spanish); Creighton, *Folklore of Lunenberg County, Nova Scotia*, pp. 140–45. An unpublished Kentucky text, learned in Oklahoma, is in the Halpert collections. The story was studied years ago by Clouston (*Popular Tales and Fictions*, II, 229–88). (H.H.)

STIFF AS A POKER

Told by Mr. Marcus Freck, Beardstown, Ill., August, 1925. He said it was regarded as a true story in Garland county, Ark., at the time of the Spanish-American War.

This item pops up every few years in various parts of the United States, and is sometimes printed in newspapers and popular magazines. A tale of old people deliberately frozen every Autumn and revived in the Spring, because their families were too poor to feed them through the Winter, was known in New England many years ago. Cf. Charles Edward Crane (*Winter in Vermont*, 1941, pp. 85–89), also B. C. Clough (*The American Imagination at Work*, 1947, pp. 331–34). The *Ford Times* (Feb., 1951, pp. 25–29) reprints the story from the *Vermont Argus and Patriot* of 1887, with a recent version entitled "Vermont's Weirdest Legend" by William Hazlett Upson. Compare Will Rice's tale of men frozen in ice like fish, then thawed out and restored to life (*Ozark Guide*, Eureka Springs, Ark., Spring, 1951, p. 50). A Little Rock newspaper (*Arkansas Gazette*, Mar. 20, 1951) carried an Associated Press account of one Marvin Baker who was "frozen stiff" but recovered after treatment in a Fayetteville, Ark., hospital. (V.R.)

An elaborately detailed New England version is in Botkin (*A Treasury of New England Folklore*, pp. 274–76). Dorson (*Jonathan Draws the Long Bow*, p. 23), in discussing the food-saving device of freezing the old people, points out that on May 8, 1852, the *Yankee Blade* said that a story of a young man who was brought to life "after having been frozen eleven months among the Alps" had been going the rounds of the press. (H.H.)

CASTING OUT THE DEVIL

Told by Mr. Sam McDaniels, White Rock, Mo., December, 1928. He heard it near Caverna, Mo., in the early days.

James D. McCabe (*Great Fortunes and How They Were Made*, 1871, pp. 554–55) tells the same story, with Peter Cartwright, pioneer Methodist preacher, as the man who called up the Devil. Gardner (*Folklore from the Schoharie Hills, New York*, 1937, pp. 37–38) relates a similar tale associated with "Ren" Dow, an evangelist who stormed through the country in the 1820's, preaching hell-fire and selling a patent medicine of his own invention. For information about this character, see Charles Coleman Sellers's biography, *Lorenzo Dow, the Bearer of the Word* (New York, 1928). (V.R.)

This is a version of Motif 1517.4, "Lover hidden in chest with feathers." To Mr. Randolph's references I should add that Sellers (*op. cit.*, pp. 202–5) gives a version of this story. He also furnished Miss Gardner (*op. cit.*, pp. 314–17) with a text of the story in ballad form, and in a personal letter to her commented that old people whom he interviewed located the story in various states. Power (*Indiana Magazine of History*, XXXVIII, 109) notes a reference to the great popularity of what is apparently this story as far back as 1817, and uses it to illustrate how journalistic copying and recopying distributed floating stories.

Other versions of this story in which Dow figures are given from the South by Hudson (*Humor of the Old Deep South*, pp. 222–24); from New York by Halpert (*New York Folklore Quarterly*, II, 94), and MacDougal (*ibid.*, III, 236–40); from Indiana by Allan M. Trout (in his column "Greetings," Louisville *Courier-*

Journal, February 13, 1951); and from Oxford, England, by Manning (*Folk-Lore,* XIV, 410–11). An unpublished text from New Jersey which does not mention Dow is in the Halpert collections. The theme of raising the devil occasionally becomes part of Type 1535, "The Rich and the Poor Peasant." See Chase (*Jack Tales,* p. 200) for an abstract from Virginia; and Fauset (*Folklore from Nova Scotia,* pp. 35–36) for a version in which the devil (i.e., the hidden lover) is raised without the motif of setting tow on fire. One version of this story, *without* the fire motif, is in the early chapbook of Friar Bacon, and, of course, antedates Lorenzo Dow by a great many years. See *The Famous Historie of Fryer Bacon,* edited by Edmund Goldsmid (Edinburgh, 1886), II, 13–18; and also Morley, *Early Prose Romances,* pp. 314–18. (H.H.)

THE BURYING OF OLD MAN KANE

Told by Mrs. Marie Wilbur, Pineville, Mo., May, 1925. She thought the yarn was "made up" by a village undertaker named Emmett, about 1915.

I used a fictionized version of this, from the same informant, in *From an Ozark Holler* (1933, pp. 55–63). Bennett Cerf (*Try and Stop Me,* 1944, pp. 198–99) tells a similar tale in which the preacher fell into the grave *under the coffin,* just as the latter was about to be lowered. In another backwoods story the central figure is a freemason, a Knight Templar with an ostrich feather in his hat and a sword round his middle. (V.R.)

In a humorous Idaho tale which lacks the motif of the curse, the gravediggers are drinking steadily and do not notice when a big Irishman falls into the grave as the coffin is being lowered. His yells scare them off. He finally crawls out from under the coffin; then sits down and finishes the whiskey jug. See Federal Writers' Project of the Work Projects Administration, *Idaho Lore,* p. 97. (H.H.)

STUCK IN A HOLLER LOG

Told by Mr. Joe Ingenthron, Forsyth, Mo., June, 1940. He got it from a Kentuckian who lived near Kissee Mills, Mo., in 1914. (V.R.)

In a Michigan lumberjack yarn given by E. C. Beck (*Lore of the Lumber Camps,* p. 333), a man who slept in a hollow log remembered the time he peeked into a schoolma'am's bedroom through the keyhole. He "felt so small he crawled out through a crack." In a version published by Selby (*100 Goofy Lies,* p. 14) a man crawls into a hollow log to escape a rain and falls asleep. He is caught when the sun begins to shrink the log. He thinks of all the mean things he has done; but when he remembers how he left his mother-in-law standing in water over her head, he felt so little he "walked straight out of the log." (H.H.)

THE ARKANSAS TRAVELER

Told by Mr. Lon Jordan, Farmington, Ark., November, 1941. Mr. Jordan said that the dialogue was only part of "a long rigamarole" which was popular many years ago. "Most of it was just silly," he said, "like the gags you hear on the radio nowadays."

The music that goes with this tale is the most famous fiddle tune in the South. There is little doubt that it was known in Arkansas in the 1850's, and perhaps earlier. Most Arkansawyers credit both the dialogue and tune to Colonel Sandford C. Faulkner (1803–74), a politician who lived in Little Rock. But the history of the piece is obscure and contradictory. See James R. Masterson (*Tall Tales of Arkansaw,* 1943, pp. 186–254, 358–82) for a fully documented discussion of this item. (V.R.)

See Catherine Marshall Vineyard (*Publications of the Texas Folklore Society,* XVIII, 11–60) for another excellent study of "The Arkansas Traveler." (H.H.)

SHE TURNED HIM INTO A PONY

Told by Mr. Clarence Keene, Pittsburg, Kan., November, 1928. He heard it near Dutch Mills, Ark., about 1900.

Several of these humorous witch-tales were circulated in the 1880's. I published a similar story in *Ozark Mountain Folks* (1932, pp. 38–41), which was reprinted in Botkin's *A Treasury of American Folklore* (1944, pp. 695–96). Compare my *Ozark Superstitions* (1947, pp. 278–79). See also Otto Ernest Rayburn (*Arkansas Historical Quarterly,* Summer, 1951, p. 212). (V.R.)

This is a combination of Motif G 241.2.1, "Witch transforms man to horse and rides him," and Motif X 31, "The dream of marking the treasure." Stories with the first motif are quite common in the American-British tradition, not as part of a dream, however, but told as actual experience. The humorous dream motif with its surprise ending is clearly the important element in this tale, and Mr. Randolph's texts are the only American examples of the second motif that I have read.

In story No. 28 in an early English jestbook (*Mery Tales, Wittie Questions and Quicke Answeres*, London [1567], reprinted by Hazlitt, *Shakespeare Jest-Books*, I, 40–42) a man tells in company of a dream he had in which the devil led him to a field to dig for gold. When the gold was found, the devil advised the man that since the gold was too heavy to carry away, he mark the spot by relieving himself over it. The man did—then woke and found "he had foul defyled his bedde." The story is retold with some changes in a 1604 jestbook (*Pasquils Jests, mixed with Mother Bunches Merriments*, in *Shakespeare Jest-Books*, III, 43). In this version the man's name is given as Mullins and the dream came when he was drunk. (H.H.)

COLONEL DOCKETT

Told by Mrs. Rose Spaulding, Eureka Springs, Ark., March, 1951. She got the story from her grandfather in the 1890's. Cf. John B. Lamar's "The Blacksmith of the Mountain Pass" in *Polly Peablossom's Wedding, and Other Tales*, edited by T. A. Burke, 1851, pp. 76–88; Lamar says that the preacher's name was Stubbleworth, the fierce blacksmith was Ned Forgerson. Lamar's tale is summarized by James H. Penrod (*Tennessee Folklore Bulletin*, XVIII, No. 4 [December, 1952], 96). See also Allsopp (*Folklore of Romantic Arkansas*, II, 1931, 11–12), who gives the fighting preacher's name as Cornelius McGuire. (V.R.)

In Pennsylvania the story of the preacher who whips a blacksmith whose practice it is to thrash Evangelical ministers is credited to Moses Dissinger, "the Lorenzo Dow of the Pennsylvania Dutch," an exponent of strenuous Christianity. The preacher and blacksmith became good friends, though it is not stated whether the latter ever joined the church. For tales about Dissinger see Brendle and Troxell (*Pennsylvania-German Folk Tales*, p. 215 ff.; for this story see pp. 222–23).

As reported from East Tennessee by Vincent (*Bert Vincent's Strolling*, pp. 9–12; reprinted in Vincent, *Us Mountain Folks*, pp. 13–18), Preacher Tom Barker, a circuit-riding Methodist known as "Ol' Sledge," licks and converts "Devil Bill" Jones, a blacksmith and rum seller.

This legend neatly demonstrates how folk tales can be used to show culture contact between regions. We know that many Pennsylvanians, including Germans, settled in the Southern Appalachians, and that the ancestors of many of the Ozark people came from the Southern Appalachians. This legend survives at the three chief points of the migration route. (H.H.)

THE WOMAN-HATER'S SON

Told by Mr. Ed Wall, Pineville, Mo., May, 1922. He heard it about 1915, from some elderly folk at Elk Springs, Mo. Otto Ernest Rayburn tells me that he heard this story at Kingston, Ark., in 1926, but the pretty girl was called "a goose" instead of "a devil red-hot from Hell." Cf. *Midwest Folklore*, II (Summer, 1952), 89–90. (V.R.)

This is Type 1678 (Motif T 371), "The Boy Who Had Never Seen a Woman." It is told by Boccaccio, in the *Decameron*, in the introduction to the fourth day. American versions have been published from North Carolina by Boggs (*Journal of American Folklore*, XLVII, 310), and South Carolina by Botkin (*A Treasury of Southern Folklore*, p. 85; reprinted from Ben Robertson, *Red Hills and Cotton*). There are unpublished versions from New Jersey and Kentucky in the Halpert collections. The story is also known in Ireland and Wales; see *Béaloideas*, VII, 177. (H.H.)

GUNPOWDER SEED

Told by Mr. Price Paine, Noel, Mo., October, 1923. He says there were many similar Indian stories which amused southwest Missourians in the 1890's. (V.R.)

Botkin (*A Treasury of New England Folklore*, p. 138) gives a

New England version in which the trader sells an Indian gunpowder, making him believe it would grow like a grain. Later the trader gives the Indian credit; when he demands repayment, the Indian tells him, "Me pay you when my powder grow." See also Dorson, *Southern Folklore Quarterly,* X (1946), 123. (H.H.)

WILLIE UP THE CHIMNEY

Told by Mr. John Chaney, Springfield, Mo., October, 1945. He had it from an aged Virginian who lived near Harrison, Ark., in the early days.

Evidently related to "Willie the Weaver," a song widely known in England and America. See Williams (*Folksongs of the Upper Thames,* 1923, p. 106), MacKenzie (*Ballads and Sea Songs from Nova Scotia,* 1928, p. 328), Sharp (*English Folk Songs from the Southern Appalachians,* 1932, I, 207–9), Brewster (*Ballads and Songs of Indiana,* 1940, p. 360), Leach and Beck (*Journal of American Folklore,* LXIII [1950], 265–66). (V.R.)

In a Bahama Negro story given by Parsons (*Folk-Tales of Andros Island, Bahamas,* p. 77) the lover hides in the chimney when the husband returns unexpectedly with a raccoon he has caught. Despite the wife's protests the husband makes a big fire to "swinge" the coon, forcing the lover to drop down. Compare the story "Casting out the Devil" for other tales in which fire is used to drive out the wife's lover. (H.H.)

HIS VOICE WAS A-CHANGING

Told by Mr. Charles S. Hiatt, Cassville, Mo., April, 1933. He got the tale from some old-timers in Barry county, Mo., and thought it might be a true story. (V.R.)

In Kentucky versions of this story, the man under the wagon has maladjusted vocal cords. Allan M. Trout published a Clinton county version in his column "Greetings," Louisville *Courier-Journal,* February 26, 1953. In an unpublished text from Crittenden county in the Halpert collections, this story is one of a cycle told about a man whose voice would shift from a high squeak to a baritone in the middle of a sentence. (H.H.)

TOO MUCH POWDER

Told by Judge J. A. Sturges, Pineville, Mo., September, 1926. He said it was well known in McDonald county, Mo., about 1889. In October, 1880, at Ponca City, Okla., according to a story by Ross Lewis (*True Magazine,* Jan., 1939, p. 67), a woman named Lizzie Merton tried to crack a safe and was killed in an explosion which wrecked the building and blew her mangled body into the street. For further information about Lizzie Merton see Anton S. Booker's *Wildcats in Petticoats* (1945, pp. 3–8). (V.R.)

A LONG-HANDLED SHOVEL

Told by Mr. Lon Jordan, Farmington, Ark., December, 1941. Mr. Jordan says the story was popular around Fayetteville, Ark., in the early 1900's. "They told it on several fellows," he said, "but I don't reckon anything like that ever really happened. It's just one of them old tales." Cf. *Southern Folklore Quarterly,* XVI (1952), 167–68. (V.R.)

This is a fool-tale version of a fairly well-known "lying tale": Type 1882, "The Man Who Fell out of a Balloon," more clearly phrased as Motif X 917, "Man falls and is buried in earth: goes for spade and digs self out." American versions show great variety in the situation in which the man is caught, and in the tools he uses to get himself out. He may be deep in earth, rock, mud, or a mudhole; caught in a snowdrift; under a log or a horse; under the ice of a river. He may need a digging tool, an axe, a pry-pole, or logs to climb out on the ice. See: Dorson, *Southern Folklore Quarterly,* VIII, 283 (Maine; logs to climb out of air hole in ice); Gardner, *Folklore from the Schoharie Hills, New York,* pp. 27–28 (reprinted from Gardner, *Journal of American Folklore,* XXVII, 305; pick and shovel); Thompson, *Body, Boots and Britches,* three New York variants, p. 61 (same as Gardner), p. 151 (shovel), p. 290 (shovel; snowdrift); Halpert, *Journal of American Folklore,* LVII, 102 (New York; pick and shovel); Huss and Werner, *Southern Folklore Quarterly,* IV, 142–43 (Florida; "Conchs": a mixed-blood group; grubbing hoe); Anderson, *Tennessee Folklore Society Bul-*

213

letin, V, 59 (Tennessee; pick); Boatright, *Tall Tales from Texas,* p. 7 (axe; chops off leg to release himself); Halpert, *Hoosier Folklore Bulletin,* I, 91–92 (Indiana; hatchet); Halpert, *California Folklore Quarterly,* IV, 251 (Montana; pole).

The Florida version, in which a man climbs a beanstalk to heaven, returns most of the way on a "platted" rope, then drops the rest of the way, resembles the version given in the early editions of Munchausen's Travels, but not found in later editions. The Baron falls, on his return from the moon, and goes for a spade to dig himself out. See the reprint of the first (1785) edition, edited by John Carswell: *Singular Travels, Campaigns, and Adventures of Baron Munchausen,* by R. E. Raspe and others (London, 1948), pp. 21–22. Scholars have mentioned the resemblance of the Munchausen story to a Serbian folktale. For an English translation of the latter story see Madam Csedomille Mijatovies, *Serbian Folk-Lore* (London, 1874), pp. 110–11. The Serbian tale continues with the boy removing his head, then going off without it. In Selby, *100 Goofy Lies,* p. 26, the man jumped headfirst from a tree, stove his head in a rock and broke it off, then had to go for a pick to dig it out. In two Irish versions (Duncan, *Folk-Lore,* IV, 189, and MacManus, *In Chimney Corners,* p. 255) the man, who was fallen deep into rock, sends his head off to get help. The Florida and Munchausen tales belong under Type 852, "The Hero Forces the Princess to Say 'That is a Lie.' " The Serbian and Irish versions are more complete forms of this Type. An incomplete text of a different version belonging to this Type was collected in Michigan by Dorson (*Western Folklore,* VIII, 131) from a Polish-born informant, and includes going home for an axe to cut himself loose, and then for a shovel to dig himself out of sand. (H.H.)

THE GREEN MAN IN THE TREE

Told by Mr. Jack Short, Galena, Mo., February, 1940. He says that "everybody in southwest Missouri" heard the tale before 1910.

Compare a similar story in Tom Moore's *Mysterious Tales and Legends of the Ozarks* (1938, pp. 19–23). Moore connects it with a local character hanged by bushwackers in the 1860's. My informant and Judge Moore lived in the same neighborhood for many years, and I believe that both men got the tale from the same source. But Moore's published version is a commonplace ghost story, while Jack Short tells it as something quite different. (V.R.)

T. Keightly (*The Fairy Mythology*, pp. 281–83; reprinted by Hartland, *English Fairy and Other Folk Tales*, pp. 132–34) quotes two old English versions of a strange story in which green people are mentioned. A boy and his sister, who resemble human beings in all respects except that "the whole surface of their skin was tinged of a green colour," were found at the mouth of certain pits. At first they ate only green beans. The boy died, but the girl got used to other food, and eventually lost her green color, was baptized, and lived in service for many years, but "was rather loose and wanton in her conduct." After she had learned English she spoke about her country where they saw no sun, but lived in a kind of twilight. All the inhabitants of her country were green in color. In the second version, her country is called St. Martin's Land.

The color green often has supernatural associations in British tradition. Green is frequently mentioned as the appropriate color of clothing for the people of elfland or fairyland, as in the ballad of "Thomas the Rhymer" (Child 37). A curious seventeenth-century broadside ballad, "Strange and True News from Westmoreland," reprinted by Ashton (*A Century of Ballads* [London, 1887], pp. 89–93) has a stranger "clothed in a bright green" appear in judgment on a man who murdered his wife. He allows the Devil to take the murderer and then departs after some parting moral admonitions to the bystanders—who decide he must have been an angel. (H.H.)

CORNBREAD AND BACON

Told by Mrs. Elizabeth Maddocks, Joplin, Mo., June, 1937. It came to her from some children near Chadwick, Mo., about 1900. (V.R.)

Botkin (*A Treasury of Southern Folklore*, p. 279) quotes a speech of Governor Jeff Davis, of Arkansas, who claimed the price of bacon was so high, "I just buy one little slice, hang it up by a long string, and let each one of my kids jump up and grease their mouths and go to bed." One of my Kentucky students told me that she had heard a joke about a poor family that hung up a fat piece of bacon, and then allowed each child to pass under it and sniff.

Thompson (*Body, Boots, and Britches*, pp. 502–3) reports a related yarn from New York as the explanation for a saying, "We'll have potatoes and pints." In Ireland people often had only potatoes to eat. If they managed to get a little piece of pork, they would suspend it over the center of the table, or set it in a dish, and then *pint* their potatoes at it. The description of a meal of potatoes alone as one of "potatoes and point" is also known in England. See *Word-Lore: The 'Folk' Magazine*, II (1927), 129, 172; III (1928), 22–23, for reports from Cornwall, Devon, and Ireland. The explanation of what goes in the center of the table varies. The discussion mentions another punning description of short rations as a meal of "bread and pull it" [pullet], and also cites Brewer's *Dictionary of Phrase and Fable* for a story of a miser who gave his boy dry bread —and whipped him for pointing it toward the cupboard where some cheese was kept. (H.H.)

SECOND SIGHT

Told by Mr. Lew Beardon, Branson, Mo., December, 1938. He heard it near Forsyth, Mo., in the 1890's, and thought it might be a true story. Cf. Stetson Kennedy *(Palmetto Country,* 1942, pp. 127–31). Reprinted by B. C. Clough *(The American Imagination at Work,* 1947, pp. 563–66). (V.R.)

This is a version of Type 1641, "Doctor Know-All." Like many other American texts of the story it is an abbreviated form, lacking Parts I and II of the complete type in which the man sets himself up as a diviner and accidentally secures the return of stolen property.This "short form" has Part III of the type form only. The false diviner's powers are tested by asking that he tell what is hidden under a receptacle. He accidentally names it by some self-pitying remark meant to admit his failure. Sometimes it is a play on his name or nickname, "Poor Robin," or "Poor Cricket"; or an

216

exclamation, such as "Merde!" In Negro versions it is often, "You've caught the old coon (i.e., himself) at last."

European and Asiatic versions of the tale were studied by Clouston *(Popular Tales and Fictions,* II, 413–31). Parsons, *Antilles,* III, 282–84, gives abstracts of eight texts as well as excellent references. Those for the United States include one Louisiana French version, and American Negro versions from Mississippi, Georgia, South Carolina, and Virginia. The following notes are supplementary. See: Mayo, *Promenade,* VI, issues 4 and 5, April–May, 1947, p. 2 (New York; Negro; from Connecticut); Speers, *Journal of American Folklore,* XXV, 284–85 (only slightly varied from Bullock, *ibid.,* XI, 13–14; Virginia; mulatto); Hurston, *Mules and Men,* pp. 111–12, and reprinted in Botkin, *A Treasury of American Folklore,* pp. 445–46 (Florida; Negro); Brewer, *Publications of the Texas Folklore Society,* X, 24–25 (Texas; Negro); Zunser, *Journal of American Folklore,* XLVIII, 160 (New Mexico; Spanish); Peixoto, *California Folklore Quarterly,* II, 31–34 (California; from Portugal); Emerson, *Tales from Welsh Wales,* pp. 186–93; *Handbook of Irish Folklore,* p. 584. Mr. Randolph's text is apparently the first to be reported from a white English-speaking narrator either in England or the United States. (H.H.)

THE FANCY POT

Told by Mr. Otto Ernest Rayburn, Eureka Springs, Ark., November, 1950. Cf. Richard M. Dorson *(Davy Crockett, American Comic Legend,* 1939, pp. 148–49). Also Botkin *(A Treasury of Western Folklore,* 1951, p. 19). (V.R.)

According to Clark *(The Rampaging Frontier,* p. 64), the enemies of Governor James B. Ray of Indiana told this yarn about him in 1825. Boatright *(Folk Laughter on the American Frontier,* pp. 54–55), who cites a version from a Crockett almanac supposedly told by Davy Crockett, says he has heard the same tale "told in the first person by more than one Southwestern frontiersman." Poley *(Friendly Anecdotes,* p. 119) tells this about a Quaker "from a backwardly community" in Pennsylvania. In an unpublished West Kentucky version in the Halpert collections, a countryman in a barber chair spit all around a cuspidor, then warned that it had better be moved or he might spit *on* it. This story, which has been in circulation in America for better than 120 years, is typical of the many yarns which mock backwoods ignorance of town refinements. Compare "Yellow Bread" in this book for another example. (H.H.)

ALF BOLEN'S HEAD

Told by Mr. Jack Short, Galena, Mo., February, 1940. He had it from his parents. The Shorts were old-timers, and they knew all about guerrilla warfare. Jack Short's mother killed a bushwhacker with an axe.

The old settlers say that Alf Bolen operated in Taney county, Mo., and Boone county, Ark., in the first years of the War between the States. He was betrayed by a woman and killed by a Federal spy, in 1863. Members of the First Iowa Cavalry stuck Bolen's head on a pole and carried it to Ozark, Mo. Uncle Sol Hembree, of Galena, Mo., told me that he saw the head on a pole at Ozark. Mary Elizabeth Mahnkey, of Kirbyville, Mo., said that Bolen's headless body was buried on a high ridge near Forsyth, Mo. Compare Tom Moore's *Mysterious Tales and Legends of the Ozarks* (1938, pp. 73–74). See also Richard Gear Hobbs *(Glamor-Land, the Ozarks,* 1944, pp. 33–34) and William Neville Collier *(Ozark and Vicinity in the Nineteenth Century,* 1946, p. 9), who says that "the head was kept on exhibition in Ozark for several days" and then sent on to Saint Louis. (V.R.)

Sergeant Anderson of the old Northwest Mounted Police cut off the head of a criminal and put it in a gunnysack in order to bring evidence back to headquarters that the man was dead. See Godsell, *Alberta Folklore Quarterly,* I, 67–68. Similarly, because of the difficulty of freighting a murdered prospector's body out of the Idaho mountains, the deputy sheriff and doctor sent to investigate the murder brought back to town only the murdered man's head. The head was treated in very cavalier fashion until it finally disappeared. See Federal Writers' Project of the Work Projects Administration, *Idaho Lore,* p. 93. (H.H.)

218

THE GIRL AND THE ROAD AGENT

Told by Dr. Leo McKellops, Anderson, Mo., May, 1933. He got the story from some neighbors near Steelville, Mo., in the early 1900's. These people were of Irish extraction, and Dr. Mc-Kellops thinks it is an old-country tale.

The theme is very close to such old ballads as "The Crafty Farmer" (Child 283), "The Yorkshire Bite," and "The Maid of Rygate." For information about these songs see Coffin *(British Traditional Ballads in North America,* 1950, pp. 151–52). Compare the "Highway Robber" song recorded by Greenleaf *(Ballads and Sea Songs of Newfoundland,* 1933, p. 47). None of these songs, so far as I know, has been reported from Missouri or Arkansas. (V.R.)

In most of the folk tale versions it is a boy who outwits the highwayman. He throws down a bag full of small coins, or something less valuable, then escapes on the robber's horse. See: Barry, *Journal of American Folklore,* XXIII, 452–54, for a version supposed to have happened in England to the father of a New England minister; Emerson, *Tales from Welsh Wales,* pp. 252–55. In several versions there is a preliminary scene in which the boy, while on his way to get money, meets the highwayman and tells him his errand. See two Isle of Skye versions, each told of the same character: MacCulloch, *Folk-Lore,* XXXIII, 383–84; Brenda MacLeod, *Tales of Dunvegan* (Stirling, 1950), pp. 87–100. Add: MacManus, *In Chimney Corners,* pp. 149–51 (Ireland). (H.H.)

PLAYED FOR A SUCKER

Told by Mr. Joe Ingenthron, Forsyth, Mo., June, 1940. Mr. Ingenthron said it was an account of an incident which occurred about 1920.

This method of dividing the catch is almost universal among the old-timers. See John F. Dunckel *(The Mollyjoggers,* n.d., p. 73), also my pamphlet *Funny Stories about Hillbillies* (1944, p. 13). Compare Fred Kniffen's "The Deer Hunt Complex in Louisiana," *Journal of American Folklore,* LXII (1949), 188, Leland Duvall's story of Arkansas deer hunters *(Arkansas Gazette,* Little Rock, Ark., Dec. 9, 1951), and an item in the Brown collection *(North Carolina Folklore,* I [1952], 261). (V.R.)

THE COWPOKES TOLD A TALE

Told by Mr. J. H. McGee, Joplin, Mo., July, 1934. He says the story was known, in several versions, to miners around Joplin in the early 1900's.

I have not seen this printed as a tale, but there is a song about it. See Larkin *(Singing Cowboy,* 1931, pp. 65–68), Lomax *(American Ballads and Folk Songs,* 1934, pp. 407–9), and Laws *(Native American Balladry,* 1950, p. 141). (V.R.)

THE THREE DREAMS

Told by Mrs. Emma L. Dusenbury, Mena, Ark., April, 1938. She got the tale from some old settlers named Cooper, in the 1880's.

Compare a similar story in Taylor Beard's *The Arkansaw Cracker Jack* (1905, p. 17). Archer Taylor *(Journal of American Folklore,* XXXIV [1921], 327–28) reports a rhymed version from St. Louis. Botkin *(A Treasury of American Folklore,* 1944, pp. 452–53) reprints some of this material. Cf. *Journal of American Folklore,* LXV (1952), 160–61. (V.R.)

This tale, Type 1626, "Dream Bread," has a world-wide distribution and has been studied by Clouston *(Popular Tales and Fictions,* II, 86–96) and Baum *(Journal of American Folklore,* XXX, 378–410). Brewster *(Hoosier Folklore Bulletin,* III, 22) gives a version he heard on a radio program, and some supplementary references. To Baum's American references should be added the items listed above by Mr. Randolph and the following: Brown, *Wit and Humor,* pp. 141–42; Landon, *Wit and Humor of the Age,* p. 448; Meier, *The Joke Tellers' Joke Book,* pp. 93–94; Parsons, *Folk-Lore of the Sea Islands, South Carolina,* pp. 68–69 (South Carolina; Negro); Pooler, *New Mexico Folklore Record,* IV, 21 (New Mexico; Spanish); Barbeau, *Journal of American Folklore,* XXXII, 178–79 (French Canadian; two texts), 179 (Ontario; two texts); Fauset, *Folklore from Nova Scotia,* p. 54

220

(Nova Scotia; Negro), pp. 54–55 (Nova Scotia; white). There is an unpublished text from New Jersey in the Halpert collections. In many of these texts some kind of meat rather than bread is the prize for the dream contest. (H.H.)

CORN FOR THE MILLER

Told by Mr. William Hatton, Columbia, Mo., July, 1929. Mr. Hatton believed that the story originated in Lawrence county, Mo., about 1905.

Variants of this item are known in many parts of the Ozark country. See Charles H. Hibler (*Down in Arkansas*, 1902, pp. 31–32) who says the tale was "hoary with age" at the turn of the century. Compare Hoenshel (*Stories of the Pioneers*, 1915, p. 36). I used one version in *Funny Stories about Hillbillies* (1944, p. 11), and referred to another in my *We Always Lie to Strangers* (1951, p. 27). Cf. *Southern Folklore Quarterly*, XVI (1952), 173–74. (V.R.)

The motif of taking everyone's advice is apparently a version of the well-known fable classified as Motif J 1041.2, "Miller, his son and the ass: trying to please everyone." For variants of the latter see Parsons, *Journal of American Folklore*, XXX, 192 (North Carolina; Negro); and the early English jestbook, *Mery Tales, Wittie Questions, and Quicke Answers*, in *Shakespeare Jest-Books*, I, 78–79. Several variants of Motif J 1874.1, "Rider takes the meal-sack on his shoulder to relieve the ass of his burden," are given in Clouston, *The Book of Noodles*, pp. 19–20. It is also tale number two in the famous chapbook of the Wise Men of Gotham, reprinted in Cunningham, *Amusing Prose Chap-Books*, pp. 24–25, and in Stapleton, *All About the Merry Tales of Gotham*, p. 17. This motif, combined with the jest of the rock in the sack as a counterweight to the meal, is in the sketch from *Down in Arkansas*, by Charles S. Hibler, quoted in Masterson, *Tall Tales of Arkansaw*, p. 275. The counterbalance theme takes a different form in the story of the stupid Swabian, in Brendle and Troxell, *Pennsylvania German Folk Tales*, p. 16. He carried a heavy object up a hill to balance a pail of water he had drawn; when he went to return the object to its place, he carried the pail of water down the hill—as a balance. (H.H.)

THE DRUMMER'S MAGIC CIRCLE

Told by Mr. Jack Short, Galena, Mo., March, 1940. He heard it about 1900. (V.R.)

The drummer's device for attempting to escape bedbugs by making a circle of molasses or tar is also utilized in versions of a tall tale. In these yarns, however, the device fails to halt the intelligent enemy. They merely take sticks or straws to cross the protecting circle. See: *Wehman's Yankee Drolleries, or, Sketches of Down-Easters*, p. 24; Loomis, *Western Folklore*, VI, 31; Hulett, *Now I'll Tell One*, p. 98; Selby, *100 Goofy Lies*, p. 6; Fauset, *Folklore from Nova Scotia*, pp. 73–74. In an Ohio text (Halpert, *Hoosier Folklore*, VII, 70), the bedbugs defeat the molasses circle by crawling up to the ceiling, then dropping on the occupants of the bed. (H.H.)

GOOD DOGS COST MONEY

Told by Mrs. Ann Miller, Aurora, Mo., February, 1948. She credits the story to a villager named Dixon. An almost identical tale was published in the monthly *Pitchfork* (Dallas, Texas, October, 1922, p. 24). (V.R.)

THREE BARRELS OF WHISKEY

Told by Mr. D. A. Hicks, Kansas City, Mo., December, 1935. He heard the tale near Hot Springs, Ark., about 1920.

Otto Ernest Rayburn (*Arcadian Magazine,* Eminence, Mo., May, 1931, pp. 18–19) printed a related story about the hog-stealers of southern Missouri; Rayburn got it from Mr. H. Vinton, who used to live in Harrison, Ark., and Hot Springs, Ark. Cf. Royal Rosamond (*Bound in This Clay,* 1945, pp. 8–9). (V.R.)

This tale is a unique version of Type 1792, "The Stingy Parson and the Slaughtered Pig." I assume Mr. Rayburn's story, mentioned by Mr. Randolph, is close to the standard form. Other versions in which the hog is stolen by the one who has advised the owner to pretend it was stolen are: Jones, *Yorker,* II, 11–12 (New York);

222

Halpert, *New York Folklore Quarterly*, II, 93 (New York); Boggs, *Journal of American Folklore*, XLVII, 313 (North Carolina). An unpublished text from New Jersey is in the Halpert collections. (H.H.)

THE BLACKSMITH'S STORY

Told by Mr. Elbert Short, Crane, Mo., July, 1933. In the early 1900's, he said, the story was known to many people near Marionville, Mo.

Compare a similar tale in Gardner (*Folklore from the Schoharie Hills, New York*, 1937, p. 65). See also the *Southern Folklore Quarterly*, XVI (1952), 172–73. (V.R.)

This is a version of Motif G 211.1.2, "Witch as horse shod with horseshoes." Gardner's note 88 to the text referred to by Mr. Randolph gives very full American and British references and other comparative notes. (H.H.)

MISTER SHARP AND THE OLD SOLDIER

Told by Mr. Lon Jordan, Farmington, Ark., December, 1941.

The first part of this piece has been printed as a legend explaining a place-name; see Marion Hughes (*Three Years in Arkansaw*, 1904, p. 90). The yarn about the two brothers appears in my *Funny Stories about Hillbillies* (1944, p. 8). (V.R.)

A related and equally convincing tale of escape from death is told in Texas and Arizona. A horse goes over the side of a canyon (in Arizona texts it is Grand Canyon) and is crushed at the foot. His rider saves himself—by getting off just before the horse reaches the ground. See Boatright, *Tall Tales from Texas*, pp. 64–65; and three Arizona texts: Boatright, *Folk Laughter on the American Frontier*, pp. 91–92; Gillmor, *University of Arizona Bulletin*, XVI, No. 1, 7–8; Botkin, *A Treasury of American Folklore*, p. 616. The last two of the Arizona versions are ascribed to John Hance, a famous guide. For the wildcat yarn add: Percy Mackaye, *Tall Tales of the Kentucky Mountains* (New York, 1926), pp. 49–56. The matching of one whopper by a greater one, as in Mr. Randolph's version, is classified as Type 1920, "Contest in Lying." (H.H.)

THE BOY THAT MADE UP SONGS

Told by Mrs. Rose Spaulding, Eureka Springs, Ark., August, 1951. Her grandfather used to tell it for the children, she says, about 1890. (V.R.)

For some discussion of the legends about fairies and other supernatural figures who give musical power to mortals, see my article, "The Devil and the Fiddle," *Hoosier Folklore Bulletin*, II, 39–43. (H.H.)

IT SURE WON'T DO NO HARM

Told by Mrs. Marie Wilbur, Pineville, Mo., March, 1929. She said it was a true story related by her stepfather, Dr. O. St. John, who practiced in the village for many years.

See a similar text in my *From an Ozark Holler* (1933, pp. 112–18). (V.R.)

RENA KILLED A STRANGER

Told by an old gentleman in McDonald county, Mo., August, 1929. He said it was a true story. Rena is dead now, and so are the Clark boys. I knew them well. If they were living, I should not publish this one. (V.R.)

DEVIL TAKE THE SKILLET

Told by Mr. Sam McDaniels, Jane, Mo., December, 1928. He heard it about 1910, from old settlers in the neighborhood.

Compare a tale entitled "Lumberman Meets the Devil," *Arcadian Life* (Caddo Gap, Ark., Oct., 1935), pp. 17–18. See also the *Southern Folklore Quarterly*, XVI (1952), 175–76. (V.R.)

There is a curious parallel to this strange yarn in an unpublished story from Crittenden county, Kentucky, in the Halpert collections. All who have moved into a certain haunted house have been frightened off by a ghost which would enter, pushing a coffin, and tell the resident to get into the coffin. One old man finally moves into the house and is heating gravy in a skillet to have with his fried meat. When the ghost comes in, the old man turns slowly around with his skillet of hot gravy—and pours it on the ghost. The story ends abruptly. (H.H.)

THE HOG-BRISTLE TRIAL

Told by Mr. Jack Short, Galena, Mo., April, 1940. He said it was the truth, and mentioned names and dates.

This yarn is widely known in Stone and Taney counties, Mo. Tom Moore *(Mysterious Tales and Legends of the Ozarks,* 1938, pp. 83–109) prints a lengthy account of the affair. According to Judge Moore's story, it was the defendant's attorney who substituted the hog-bristles for the plaintiff's whiskers. I knew this lawyer well, and he did not deny the truth of Moore's version. Other persons in the neighborhood, however, say that the foreman of the jury, or even the judge, may have been responsible. (V.R.)

I am certain I have read other versions of this "true" story, but cannot recall where. A variation on the theme is reported from New York by Thompson *(Body, Boots and Britches,* p. 167). A justice of the peace was on trial for pulling a farmer's beard in a dispute over a hoss-trade. When asked for his defense, he looked at the farmer and said, "Was it your whiskers I pulled? I thought I had hold of the horse's tail." (H.H.)

TOO MUCH CHURCH WORK

Told by Mr. George Head, Eureka Springs, Ark., April, 1951. Amy Johnson Miller *(The Pioneer Doctor in the Ozarks White River Country,* 1947, pp. 80–81) spins the same yarn, which she credits to a traveling salesman.

Bennett Cerf *(Saturday Review of Literature,* Sept. 1, 1951, p. 5) has a modern version of this one, with "political activity" instead of "church work," and the governor taking the preacher's place. Cf. *Southern Folklore Quarterly,* XVI (1952), 174–75. (V.R.)

This appears to be a modern version of a standard fool tale: Motif J 2412.4, "Imitation of diagnosis by observation: ass's flesh." In the European form, and also in New Jersey, the new practitioner deduces the patient ate too much mule—because there is a saddle under the bed. (H.H.)

THE STOLEN WEDGES

Told by Mr. Rufe Scott, Galena, Mo., October, 1944. Judge Scott had it from his father, who lived near Hurley, Mo., in the early days.

Lorenzo Dow (1777–1834), known as "Crazy Ren," was a wandering preacher who sold patent medicine as a side line. Charles Coleman Sellers's biography *Lorenzo Dow, the Bearer of the Word* (New York, 1928) presents a wealth of information about this character. See Emelyn Gardner *(Folklore from the Schoharie Hills, New York, 1937, p. 317)* for a reference to Dow's success in detecting criminals. (V.R.)

This tale belongs under Motif J 1141, "Confession obtained by ruse." It is one of the classic thief-catching tales ascribed to Lorenzo Dow. Usually when Dow is requested to find a thief (the property stolen varies in the different stories) he picks up a stone on the way to the meetinghouse. Sometimes he says he knows and will hit the thief; sometimes that God has decreed he will hit the guilty man. He makes the gesture of throwing, and the guilty person involuntarily gives himself away, usually by some movement.

It is a stolen axe in a version from New Jersey by Beck *(New York Folklore Quarterly, IV, 47–48)*, and the guilty man ducks; a stolen axe in Oxfordshire, England, in Manning *(Folk-Lore, XIV, 211–12)*, and the man tries to hide behind a pillar; a stolen donkey in a Maryland tale by Sellers *(op. cit., pp. 149–50)*, and the thief ducks his head below the pew. In a North Carolina version by Boggs *(Journal of American Folklore, XLVII, 313)* the preacher, who is not named, says he will throw two rocks and hit the sheep thief, and a man yells out his confession of guilt.

In another version given by Sellers *(op. cit., pp. 150–51)*, an axe has been stolen, and Dow says the guilty man is in the congregation and at that moment has a small feather on his nose. The thief moves his hand to brush off the nonexistent feather; then confesses. In another Oxfordshire story given by Manning *(Folk-Lore, XIV,*

226

412), Dow utters a curse on the thief's household which will take effect unless the stolen pig is returned by the next day. The pig is returned, but the thief is detected in the process.

Obviously the personality of the speaker conveyed a conviction that his curse would be effective. The same forcefulness must have been evident in a certain Dr. Roberts, the New York "wizard of Remsen." According to Roberts (New York Folklore Quarterly, III, 44–45), the doctor was requested to help recover a set of double harness. He called together all the dissolute characters within a radius of several miles, ushered them into one room, and invited them to be seated. He explained that one of them had stolen the harness. "Now, when I count three, I want every one of you to stand up; and if the one who stole the harness stands up, he will immediately fall dead." When he had counted three, all stood up but one man.

Other preachers before Dow have been called on to catch thieves. In several old English jestbooks, a man who has had a goose stolen asks the priest or curate for help. In church the priest orders the congregation to sit down. When they have, he asks why they aren't all sitting. They protest that they are. The curate says, "He who stole the goose isn't sitting." Man says, "But I do"—thus giving himself away. See Mery Tales, Wittie Questions, and Quicke Answers (1567) reprinted in Shakespeare Jest-Books, I, 102; Certayne Conceyts and Jeasts (1614), in Shakespeare Jest-Books, III, 4. The story is adapted to find a pie-stealer in The Pleasant Conceites of Old Hobson, The Merry Londoner (1607), in Shakespeare Jest-Books, III, 41, with the difference that old Hobson gets his servants drunk in order to lower the thief's guard.

Obviously Dow's success in catching thieves made him the center for such stories, many of which had probably been in circulation long before his time. The story of the rooster that is to crow from beneath a sooty pot when the guilty man touches the pot is an old one. The rooster remains silent; but the guilty man is caught because he has clean hands, not having dared to touch the pot. See notes to "The Poppet Caught a Thief," in Randolph, Who Blowed Up the Church House?, p. 210, for references to versions from

227

Arkansas, Mississippi, and Newfoundland. In New York, Roberts *(New York Folklore Quarterly,* III, 45–46) reports this of another thief catcher, Dr. Roberts, the "wizard of Remsen." According to Sellers *(op. cit.,* p. 149), in Virginia the trick is ascribed to Lorenzo Dow.

It might be worth noting here that this rooster-under-the-pot trick is based on an actual folk belief that has been practiced quite seriously. Hunt *(Popular Romances of the West of England,* pp. 421–22) gives a tale from Cornwall in which a cock does crow when the guilty woman touches the brandice (baking vessel) placed over it. The woman faints, then confesses the theft. Botkin *(Lay My Burden Down,* p. 49) gives another form of this test, without the pot, from Georgia Negroes. An old man and woman are proved to be thieves because they refuse to touch the head of a rooster protruding from its coop. In this test, as in the versions above, the rooster is supposed to indicate the guilty parties by crowing.

Another thief-catching story, given by Brendle and Troxell *(Pennsylvania German Folk Tales,* pp. 181–82), is rather like the rooster-under-the-pot trick. Each man's innocence is to be tested by rubbing his hands on a donkey's tail; the donkey is to bray when the thief touches his tail. The master has previously rubbed balsam on the tail. One man whose hands remain free of the smell of balsam is thus self-convicted. (H.H.)

BABES IN THE WOODS

Told by Mrs. Emma L. Dusenbury, Mena, Ark., April, 1938. She first heard it from her neighbors, about 1885.

Doubtless related to the well-known British song, printed in Percy's *Reliques* and many later collections. For local texts see Belden *(Ballads and Songs,* 1940, pp. 106–7), also my *Ozark Folksongs* (I, 1946, pp. 365–68). Frank L. Beals *(Backwoods Baron,* 1951, p. 74) reports a fragmentary prose version from Carroll county, Ark. Cf. *Journal of American Folklore,* LXV (1952), 165. (V.R.)

A prose form of this story entitled "The Babes in the Woods" was published, together with "The History of Cinderella, or The

228

Little Glass Slipper," in a Glasgow chapbook reprinted in John Cheap, *The Chapman's Library*. This chapbook version follows the story of the long broadside ballad quite closely, though with some omissions and additions. The softer-hearted one of two ruffians hired by the children's uncle abandons them instead of murdering them, though he has to stab his companion in order to let them live. They wander in the woods eating blackberries, waiting in vain for the man to return with cakes to feed them, and starve to death that night. Years later their bodies are found, covered with unwithered leaves, and watched by a Robin Redbreast. "Many gentle hearts" think the robin brought the leaves which made their grave. (H.H.)

Bibliography of Works Cited

Aarne, Antti, and Stith Thompson. The Types of the Folk-Tale. Helsinki, 1928. Folklore Fellows Communications, No. 74. Cited as Type.

Adams, Joey. From Gags to Riches. New York, 1949.

Addy, Sidney Oldall. Household Tales with Other Traditional Remains. London and Sheffield, 1895.

Alford, Violet. Introduction to English Folklore. London, 1952.

Allsopp, Fred W. Folklore of Romantic Arkansas. 2 vols. New York, 1931.

Anecdota Americana. New York, 1934.

Ashton, John. A Century of Ballads. London, 1887.

Aubrey, John. Miscellanies upon Various Subjects. 4th ed. London, 1857.

Beals, Frank L. Backwoods Baron. Wheaton, Ill., 1951.

Beard, Taylor. The Arkansaw Cracker Jack. Chicago, 1905.

Beck, Earl C. Lore of the Lumber Camps. Ann Arbor, Mich., 1948.

Belden, H. M. Ballads and Songs. Columbia, Mo., 1940.

Bett, Henry. English Legends. 2nd ed. London and New York, 1952.

Black, George Fraser, and Northcote W. Thomas. Examples of Printed Folk-Lore concerning the Orkney and Shetland Islands. London, 1903. Publications of the Folk-Lore Society, Vol. XLIX.

Boatright, Mody C. Folk Laughter on the American Frontier. New York, 1949.

———— Gib Morgan, Minstrel of the Oil Fields. Austin, Texas, 1945.

———— Tall Tales from Texas. Dallas, Texas, 1934.

231

Booker, Anton S. Wildcats in Petticoats. Girard, Kan., 1945.

Botkin, B. A. Lay My Burden Down. Chicago, 1945.

—— A Treasury of American Folklore. New York, 1944.

—— A Treasury of New England Folklore. New York, 1947.

—— A Treasury of Southern Folklore. New York, 1949.

—— A Treasury of Western Folklore. New York, 1951.

Brand, John. Observations on the Popular Antiquities of Great Britain. A new edition arranged by Sir Henry Ellis. 3 vols. London, 1849.

Brendle, Thomas R., and William S. Troxell. Pennsylvania German Folk Tales, Legends, Once-Upon-a-Time Stories, Maxims, and Sayings. Norristown, Pa., 1944.

Brewster, Paul G. Ballads and Songs of Indiana. Bloomington, Ind., 1940.

Brown, Marshall. Wit and Humor. Chicago, 1880.

Bryan, William S., and Robert Rose. Pioneer Families of Missouri. St. Louis, 1876.

Burke, T. A. (ed.). Polly Peablossom's Wedding, and Other Tales. Philadelphia, 1851.

Burne, Charlotte Sophia, and Georgina P. Jackson. Shropshire Folk-Lore. London, 1883.

Campbell, J. F. Popular Tales of the West Highlands. 4 vols. Paisley, 1890–93.

Campbell, John Gregorson. Clan Traditions and Popular Tales of the Western Highlands and Islands. London, 1895.

Carmer, Carl. Stars Fell on Alabama. New York, 1934.

Carrière, Joseph M. Tales from the French Folklore of Missouri. Evanston, Ill., 1937.

Carswell, John (ed.). Singular Travels, Campaigns, and Adventures of Baron Munchausen. London, 1948.

Cerf, Bennett. Try and Stop Me. New York, 1944.

Chambers, Robert. Popular Rhymes of Scotland. London and Edinburgh, 1870.

Chase, Richard. Grandfather Tales. Boston, 1948.

—— The Jack Tales; with an Appendix Compiled by Herbert Halpert. Cambridge, Mass., 1943.

232

Cheap, John. The Chapman's Library; the Scottish Chap Literature of the Last Century Classified. 3 vols. Glasgow, 1877–78.

Choice Notes from *Notes and Queries:* Folk-Lore. London, 1859.

Clark, Thomas D. The Rampaging Frontier. Indianapolis and New York, 1939.

Clough, Ben C. The American Imagination at Work. New York, 1947.

Clouston, W. A. The Book of Noodles. London, 1888.

———— Popular Tales and Fictions. 2 vols. Edinburgh and London, 1887.

Coffin, Tristram P. The British Traditional Ballad in America. Philadelphia, 1950.

Collier, William Neville. Ozark and Vicinity in the Nineteenth Century. Long Beach, Calif., 1946.

Collins, Earl A. Folk Tales of Missouri. Boston, 1935.

———— Legends and Lore of Missouri. San Antonio, Texas, 1951.

Crane, Charles Edward. Winter in Vermont. New York, 1941.

Creighton, Helen. Folklore of Lunenberg County, Nova Scotia. Ottawa, 1950. National Museum of Canada Bulletin, No. 117.

Croy, Homer. What Grandpa Laughed At. New York, 1948.

Cunningham, Robert Hays. Amusing Prose Chap-Books. London and Glasgow, 1889.

Curtin, Jeremiah. Irish Folk-Tales, edited by Seamus O'Duilearga. Dublin, 1943.

Cutting, Edith E. Lore of an Adirondack County. Ithaca, N.Y., 1944.

Dorrance, Ward Allison. Three Ozark Streams. Richmond, Mo., 1937.

Dorson, Richard M. Davy Crockett, American Comic Legend. New York, 1939.

———— Jonathan Draws the Long Bow. Cambridge, Mass., 1946.

Dunckel, John F. The Mollyjoggers. Springfield, Mo., c. 1908.

Elgart, J. M. Over Sixteen. New York, 1951.

Elzey, W. H. Things About Things. Eureka Springs, Ark., c. 1946.

Emerson, Peter Henry. Tales from Welsh Wales. London, 1894.

Fauset, Arthur Huff. Folklore from Nova Scotia. New York,

233

1931. Memoirs of the American Folklore Society, Vol. XXIV.

Fletcher, John Gould. Arkansas. Chapel Hill, N.C., 1947.

Flower, Robin. The Western Island, or the Great Blasket. New York, 1945.

Fortier, Alcée. Louisiana Folk-Tales. New York, 1895. Memoirs of the American Folklore Society, Vol. II.

Funny Side Up. New York, 1952.

Gard, Robert E. Johnny Chinook. London, New York, and Toronto, 1945.

Gardner, Emelyn E. Folklore from the Schoharie Hills, New York. Ann Arbor, Mich., 1937.

Goldsmid, Edmund. The Famous Historie of Fryer Bacon. Edinburgh, 1886.

Gore, E. K., and E. A. C. Speare. New Hampshire Folk Tales. Plymouth, N.H., 1932.

Greenleaf, Elisabeth B., and Grace Yarrow Mansfield. Ballads and Sea Songs of Newfoundland. Cambridge, Mass., 1933.

Greenough, William Parker. Canadian Folk-Life and Folk-Lore. New York, 1897.

Grice, Frederick. Folk Tales of the North Country, Drawn from Northumberland and Durham. London and Edinburgh, 1951.

Gutch, Eliza. Examples of Printed Folk-Lore concerning the North Riding of Yorkshire, York and the Ainsty. London, 1901. Publications of the Folk-Lore Society, Vol. XLV.

Gutch, Eliza, and Mabel Peacock. Examples of Printed Folklore concerning Lincolnshire. London, 1908. Publications of the Folk-Lore Society, Vol. LXVIII.

Halliwell, James Orchard. Popular Rhymes and Nursery Tales. London, 1849.

Handbook of Irish Folklore, see O'Súilleabháin, Seán.

Hardwick, Charles. Traditions, Superstitions, and Folklore: Chiefly Lancashire and the North of England. Manchester and London, 1872.

Hartland, Edwin Sidney. English Fairy and Other Folk Tales. London, 1890.

———— The Science of Fairy Tales. 2nd ed. London, 1925.

234

Hazlitt, W. Carew. Shakespeare Jest-Books. 3 vols. London, 1864.
Henderson, William. Notes on the Folklore of the Northern Counties of England and the Borders. London, 1879.
Hertz, Emmanuel. Lincoln Talks. New York, 1939.
Hibler, Charles H. Down in Arkansas. New York, 1902.
Hobbs, Richard Gear. Glamor-Land, the Ozarks. Manhattan, Kan., 1944.
Hoenshel, E. J., and L. S. Hoenshal. Stories of the Pioneers. Branson, Mo., 1915.
House, Boyce. Tall Talk from Texas. San Antonio, Texas, 1944.
Hudson, Arthur Palmer. Humor of the Old Deep South. New York, 1936.
Hughes, Marion. Three Years in Arkansaw. Chicago, 1904.
Hulett, O. C. Now I'll Tell One. Chicago, 1935.
Hunt, Robert. Popular Romances of the West of England. 3rd ed. London, 1881.
Hurston, Zora Neale. Mules and Men. Philadelphia, 1935.
Jackson, Thomas W. Through Missouri on a Mule. Chicago, 1946. (First ed. appeared in 1904.)
Jacobs, Joseph. English Fairy Tales. 2nd ed. New York and London, 1893.
———— More English Fairy Tales. London, 1894.
Jagendorf, M. A. Sand in the Bag, and Other Folk Stories of Ohio, Indiana, and Illinois. New York, 1952.
Johnson, Clifton. What They Say in New England. Boston, 1896.
Johnson, Guy B. Folk-Culture on St. Helena Island, South Carolina. Chapel Hill, N.C., 1930.
Jones, W. H., and L. L. Kropf. The Folk-Tales of the Magyars. London, 1889.
Kempt, Robert. The American Joe Miller: a Collection of Yankee Wit and Humor. London, 1865.
Kennedy, Patrick. The Fireside Stories of Ireland. Dublin, 1870.
———— Legendary Fictions of the Irish Celts. London, 1866.
Kennedy, Stetson. Palmetto Country. New York, 1942.
Landon, Melville D. Wit and Humor of the Age. Chicago, 1901.
Larkin, Margaret. Singing Cowboy. New York, 1931.

Laws, G. Malcolm. Native American Balladry. Philadelphia, 1950.
Leather, Ella M. The Folk-Lore of Herefordshire. Hereford and London, 1912.
Lockridge, Norman. Waggish Tales of the Czechs. Chicago, 1947.
Lomax, John A., and Alan Lomax. American Ballads and Folk Songs. New York, 1934.
Lummis, Charles F. The Land of Poco Tiempo. New York, 1925.
McCabe, James D. Great Fortunes and How They Were Made. Cincinnati, Ohio, 1871.
Mackaye, Percy. Tall Tales of the Kentucky Mountains. New York, 1926.
MacKenzie, W. R. Ballads and Sea Songs from Nova Scotia. Cambridge, Mass., 1928.
MacLeod, Brenda. Tales of Dunvegan. Stirling, 1950.
MacManus, Seumas. Donegal Fairy Stories. New York, 1919.
———— The Donegal Wonder Book. Philadelphia, 1926.
———— In Chimney Corners. New York, 1899.
———— The Well o' the World's End. New York, 1939.
Masterson, James R. Tall Tales of Arkansaw. Boston, 1943.
Meier, Frederick. The Joke Tellers' Joke Book. Philadelphia, 1944.
Mijatovies, Madam Csedomille. Serbian Folk-Lore. London, 1874.
Miller, Amy Johnson. The Pioneer Doctor in the Ozarks White River Country. Kansas City, Mo., 1947.
Moore, Tom. Mysterious Tales and Legends of the Ozarks. Philadelphia, 1938.
Morley, Henry. Early Prose Romances. The Carisbrooke Library, IV. London, 1889.
Morris, Lucile. Bald Knobbers. Caldwell, Idaho, 1939.
Morris, Robert L. "Told in Ozarkia," in Folk-Say. Norman, Okla., 1931.
Motif, see Thompson, Stith, Motif-Index of Folk-Literature.
Mumey, Nolie. The Life of Jim Baker. Denver, Colo., 1931.
Münchausen, Baron. The Travels of Baron Münchausen. Edited by William Rose. London and New York, n.d. Broadway Translations. See Carswell, John.

236

Musick, John R. Stories of Missouri. New York, 1897.

Neely, Charles, and John Webster Spargo. Tales and Songs of Southern Illinois. Menasha, Wis., 1938.

New Hampshire's Daughters, Folk-Lore Committee. Folk-Lore Sketches and Reminiscences of New Hampshire Life. Boston, 1910.

Northall, George F. English Folk-Rhymes. London, 1892.

Oklahoma, a Guide to the Sooner State. Norman, Okla., 1941.

O'Súilleabháin, Seán. A Handbook of Irish Folklore. Dublin, 1942. Cited as *Handbook of Irish Folklore.*

Ozark Guide. Ed. by Otto Ernest Rayburn, Eureka Springs, Ark., 1943—. Several issues of this quarterly magazine are cited in the notes.

Parsons, Elsie Clews. Folk-Lore of the Antilles. 3 vols. New York, 1933, 1936, 1943. Memoirs of the American Folklore Society, Vol. XXVI. Cited as Parsons, *Antilles.*

———— Folk-Lore of the Sea Islands, South Carolina. Cambridge, Mass., and New York, 1923. Memoirs of the American Folklore Society, Vol. XVI.

———— Folk-Tales of Andros Island, Bahamas. New York, 1918. Memoirs of the American Folklore Society, Vol. XIII.

Peele, George. The Old Wives' Tale. In the Malone Society Reprints, ed. by Horace Hart. London, 1909.

Poley, Irvin C., and Ruth V. Poley. Friendly Anecdotes. New York, 1950.

Puckett, N. N. Folk Beliefs of the Southern Negro. Chapel Hill, N.C., 1926.

Randolph, Vance. From an Ozark Holler. New York, 1933.

———— Funny Stories about Hillbillies. Girard, Kan., 1944.

———— Funny Stories from Arkansas. Girard, Kan., 1943.

———— Ozark Folksongs. 4 vols. Columbia, Mo., 1946–50.

———— Ozark Ghost Stories. Girard, Kan., 1944.

———— Ozark Mountain Folks. New York, 1932.

———— The Ozarks. New York, 1931.

———— Ozark Superstitions. New York, 1947.

Randolph, Vance. We Always Lie to Strangers. New York, 1951.

Randolph, Vance. Who Blowed Up the Church House? and Other Ozark Folk-tales. New York, 1952.

Rayburn, Otto Ernest. Ozark Country. New York, 1941.

———— Rayburn's Roadside Chats. Beebe, Ark., 1939.

Reynard, Elizabeth. The Narrow Land, Folk Chronicles of Old Cape Cod. Boston and New York, 1934.

Richardson, Ethel Park. American Mountain Songs. New York, 1927.

Robertson, Ben. Red Hills and Cotton; an Upcountry Memory. New York, 1942.

Rosamond, Royal. Bound in This Clay. Oklahoma City, Okla., 1945.

Sandburg, Carl. The People, Yes. New York, 1936.

Saxon, Lyle, and others. Gumbo Ya-Ya. Boston, 1945.

Schermerhorn, James. Schermerhorn's Stories. New York, 1928.

Selby, E. E. 100 Goofy Lies. Decatur, Ill. c. 1939.

Sellers, Charles Coleman. Lorenzo Dow, the Bearer of the Word. New York, 1928.

Seymour, St. John D. Irish Witchcraft and Demonology. Baltimore, 1913.

Shakespeare Jest-Books. See Hazlitt, W. Carew.

Sharp, Cecil. English Folksongs from the Southern Appalachians. 2 vols. London, 1932.

Shoemaker, Henry W. Mountain Minstrelsy of Pennsylvania. Philadelphia, 1931.

Sikes, W. British Goblins. Boston, 1881.

Smith, H. Allen. The Compleat Practical Joker. New York, 1953.

Spurlock, Pearl. Over the Old Ozark Trails. Branson, Mo., 1936.

Stapleton, Alfred. All About the Merry Tales of Gotham. Nottingham, 1900.

Stead, Christina. Letty Fox. New York, 1946.

Taliaferro, H. E. Fisher's River (North Carolina) Scenes and Characters. New York, 1859.

Thomas, Lowell. Tall Stories. New York, 1945. (First published in 1931.)

238

Thompson, Harold W. Body, Boots and Britches. Philadelphia, 1940.

Thompson, Stith. The Folktale. New York, 1946.

——— Motif-Index of Folk-Literature. 6 vols. Bloomington, Ind., 1932–36. Cited as Motif.

Thorp, N. Howard (Jack). Tales of the Chuck Wagon. Santa Fe, N.M., 1926.

Thorp, N. Howard (Jack), and Neil M. Clark. Pardner of the Wind. Caldwell, Idaho, 1945.

Type, see Aarne and Thompson.

United States. Work Projects Administration, Federal Writers' Project. Idaho Lore. Caldwell, Idaho, 1939.

——— South Carolina Folk Tales. Columbia, S.C., 1941.

Vestal, Stanley. Queen of the Cow Towns. New York, 1952.

Vincent, Bert. Bert Vincent's Strolling. Knoxville, Tenn., 1940.

——— Here in Tennessee. Knoxville, Tenn., 1945.

——— Us Mountain Folks. Knoxville, Tenn., 1945.

Wehman's Yankee Drolleries, or, Sketches of Down-Easters. New York, n.d.

Weiss, Harry B. A Book about Chapbooks. Trenton, N.J., 1942.

White, Newman Ivey, and others. The Frank C. Brown Collection of North Carolina Folklore. 3 vols. Durham, N.C., 1952–54.

Whitney, A. W. and C. C. Bullock. Folklore of Maryland. New York, 1925. Memoirs of the American Folklore Society, Vol. XVIII.

Williams, Alfred. Folk-Songs of the Upper Thames. London, 1923.

Wilson, Charles Morrow. Backwoods America. Chapel Hill, N.C., 1934.

Withers, Carl. A Rocket in My Pocket. New York, 1948.

Woodruff, Press. A Backwoods Philosopher from Arkansaw. Chicago, 1901.

Wright, Elizabeth Mary. Rustic Speech and Folk-Lore. London, 1913.